GLAM

G L A M

THE

PERFORMANCE

OF

STYLE

First published 2013 by order of the Tate Trustees
by Tate Liverpool
Albert Dock, Liverpool Waterfront, L3 4BB
in association with
Tate Publishing, a division of Tate Enterprises Ltd,
Millbank, London SW1P 4RG
www.tate.org.uk/publishing

on the occasion of the exhibition
Glam! The Performance of Style
Tate Liverpool
8 February to 12 May 2013

This exhibition is organised in collaboration
with Schirn Kunsthalle Frankfurt, and Lentos Kunstmuseum Linz

Schirn Kunsthalle Frankfurt
14 June to 22 September 2013
Lentos Kunstmuseum Linz
19 October to 2 February 2014

Culture

With the support of the Culture Programme of the European Union
Supported by Tate Liverpool Members and the Glam! Supporters Group

*This project has been funded with support from the European Commission.
This publication reflects the views only of the author, and the Commission cannot be
held responsible for any use which may be made of the information contained therein.*

A catalogue record for this book is available from the British Library

ISBN 978-1-849760-92-8

Distributed in the United States and Canada by ABRAMS, New York
Library of Congress Control Number: applied for

Designed by Secondary Modern, London
Printed by Graphicom, Italy
Cover image: Franz Gertsch *Marina making up Luciano* 1975

CONTENTS

FOREWORD

The glam era of the early 1970s has an enduring appeal, with the music and outlandish styles of styles of the period remaining influential today. The period has also attracted renewed interest over recent years, with many historians finding compelling parallels between contemporary experience and the socio-cultural circumstances of the early 1970s. Long regarded as a stylistic aberration, glam has also experienced an unprecedented revival, its expression and concerns being rediscovered and regenerated through the innovations of contemporary artists, stylists and filmmakers. Moving beyond nostalgia, the exhibition *Glam! The Performance of Style* is the first ever exhibition to trace the genealogy of glam to the spirit of creative freedom evident in the British Art schools of the 1960s and the phenomenon of camp that emerged in the New York underground art scene during the same period. It explores how the realms of fine art, music, fashion and performance converged, with the personification of the artwork being adopted as an artistic strategy, whilst major artists also exploring ideas of theatricality, androgyny, irony, dandyism, and visual excess. This publication, like the exhibition that inspired it, reveals the absorption of these fine art ideas at the long-front of popular culture.

We would firstly like to thank all of the lenders to the exhibition who have agreed to part with much valued works for the duration of the show, as well as the key figures, curators and historians who have been generous enough to share their knowledge and expertise during the evolution of the exhibition. In particular, we would like to acknowledge Martin Barden; Bryan Biggs; Michael Bracewell; Marc Camille Chaimowicz; Stuart Comer; Duggie Fields; William Fowler; Paul Gorman; Christoph Grunenberg; Joe E. Jeffreys; Allen Jones; Marco Livingstone; Chrissie Iles; Juliet Mann; Lynda Morris; Zandra Rhodes; Russell Roberts; Jon Savage; Rupert Smith; Steven Thomas; Keith at Smile; Judith Watt, and Val Williams. We would also like to thank a number of individuals who have provided valuable guidance during our planning, in particular Anne Barz, Kunsthalle Hamburg; June Bateman, June Bateman Fine Art, New York; Chris Bishop; Russell Bowman; Jeremy Deller; Stella Keen; Paul Kennedy; Astrid Proll and Paul Reeves. We are very grateful for the guest authors in this book for contributing their own scholarship and knowledge, enabling us to throw fresh light on this fascinating era.

In particular we would like to thank Darren Pih for his dedication to this ambitious and original project. From its inception to delivery he has worked tirelessly to uncover the story of glam and its relationship to the fine art of the period. His essay in this publication gives some indication of his passion for, and knowledge of, this area. As ever, we would like to express our thanks to the team of dedicated staff at Tate Liverpool, particularly Eleanor Clayton, Assistant Curator, who was instrumental in helping us to realise the exhibition and accompanying publication. We are also grateful to Sivan Amar, Ken Simons and Barry Bentley for efficiently running the complex shipping and installation processes; Roger Sinek for his technical expertise; and our team of conservators, as well as a number of other Tate Liverpool staff, including Jemima Pyne, Ian Malone, and Ami Guest for their tremendous support in creating this publication and Maria Percival for thoughtfully curating the complex interpretation for the show.

During the development of the exhibition we have benefited from the research input and energies of the Winchester School of Art, and would like to thank Jonathan Harris, Jonathan Faiers, John Hopkins, August Davis and Oliver Gilbert for their enthusiasm, critical advice and contribution.

We are delighted to have as tour partners Schirn Kunsthalle Frankfurt and Lentos Kunstmuseum Linz, and would like to thank our colleagues there, especially Max Hollein, Inka Drögemüller, Esther Schlicht and Matthias Ulrich in Frankfurt, and Stella Rollig and Magnus Hoffmüller in Linz, for their collaboration. We are grateful for the generous support of Maria Rus Bojan from MB Art Agency, Amsterdam, and Melle Hendrikse for their invaluable contribution to this project. This exhibition has been made possible by the provision of insurance through the Government Indemnity Scheme. Tate would like to thank H M Government for providing Government Indemnity and the Department for Culture, Media and Sport and the Arts Council England for arranging the indemnity.

Last, but certainly not least, we would like to express our sincerest gratitude to the Culture Programme of the European Union for their major support of the exhibition, and symposium *Glamorama*. Collectively, the programme and publication provide a critical reflection on a fascinating period for both fine art and popular culture, whilst evoking the enduring allure of this flamboyant era. We would like to thank Fiona Deuss-Frandi for all her support for this project, and also Gaby Styles and Sue Grindrod at Tate Liverpool and their teams for leading the process for this grant which has benefited all three participating institutions.

FRANCESCO MANACORDA
Artistic Director
Tate Liverpool

ANDREA NIXON
Executive Director
Tate Liverpool

LIST of LENDERS

A number of institutions, galleries and individuals have supported this exhibition by lending works from their collection. In particular, we would like to thank:

Valerie Allan;
AA Bronson, New York/Toronto;
Adam the Second (the late Paul Cotton);
Steven Arnold Archive;
Estate of Evelyne Axell;
Bamalama Posters;
Anne Bean;
Celia Birtwell;
Derek Boshier;
British Film Institute;
Broadway 1602, New York;
The Estate of Guy Bourdin;
Galerie Buchholz, Cologne;
Kevin Cann;
Cheim & Reid, New York;
Roger Crimlis;
John and Molly Dove;
Liz Eggleston;
Electronic Arts Intermix, New York;
Fales Library & Special Collections, New York University;
Richard L. Feigen & Co., New York;
Harry Feld;
Harry Gamboa Jr;
Henrique Faria Fine Art, New York;
Bryan Ferry;
Gladstone Gallery, New York;
Paul Gorman;
Michael Hoppen Gallery, London;
Steven Kasher Gallery, New York;
Leandro Katz;
Kunsthalle zu Keil;
Jürgen Klauke, Cologne;
Johan Kugelberg / Boo-Hooray Gallery;
Liebelt Collection, Hamburg;
Andrew Logan;
Cary Loren;
Ludwig Museum – Museum of Contemporary Art, Budapest;
Matthew Marks Gallery, New York;
Bruce McLean;
Metro Pictures, New York;
Migros Museum für Gegenwartskunst, Zurich;
Rumi Missabu
Jan Mot and Sprüth Magers London;
The Gallery Mourmans, Maastricht;

Museum of London;
Museum of Modern Art, New York;
Niagara;
North West Film Archive;
Pace/McGill, New York;
Martin Parr;
Anton Perich;
The Redfern Gallery, London;
Mick Rock, New York;
Royal College of Art, London;
Musée d'art Moderne, Saint-Étienne Metropole;
Paul Richards;
The Sander Collection, Darmstadt;
Jon Savage;
Esther Schipper, Berlin;
Peter Schlesinger, New York;
Karl Stoecker, Miami;
'Exotic' Adrian Street;
Billy Sullivan, New York;
UCLA Chicano Studies Research Centre, Los Angeles;
Ulay;
Victoria & Albert Museum, London;
The Andy Warhol Museum, Pittburgh;
Michael Werner Gallery, New York;
Whitworth Art Gallery, University of Manchester;
Wilkinson Gallery, London;

as well as lenders who would prefer to remain anonymous.

The Politics of Artifice

Darren Pih

A defining characteristic of art-historical and cultural narrative is the revival of or allusion to past styles and eras. Often triggered by historians who find parallels in historical circumstance or instigated by the innovations of artists who rediscover and regenerate stylistic approaches from the past, in recent years the stylistic residue and culture of the 1970s has been subject to new attention and revisionary scholarship. In particular, historians have increasingly identified blind spots in the traditional narrative that posits 1970s Britain as experiencing a post-1960s hangover, locked in socio-economic declinism, a society hamstrung by industrial disputes. If 1970s Britain was such a dead-end, how was it able to produce such a vibrancy of pop music, film and fashion? Why have its styles and tastes been repeatedly revived, continuing to find purchase in the contemporary imagination?

Nice Style
Pre-Performance Pose, at Sonia Henie Niels Onstad Foundation, Oslo 1972
Photograph, colour, on paper

One particular aspect of 1970s popular culture has been especially susceptible to this cycle of remaking and remodelling of the past: the phenomenon of 'glam'. A pop abbreviation of 'glamour' (and a term first used in 1937), glam found its primary expression in fashion, applied arts, film and photography and – most explicitly – through pop music, exploding across in Britain during the years 1971 to 1975. Glam is characterised by its use of stylistic overstatement, revelling in revivalism, irony, theatricality, and androgyny, privileging surface effect and artifice over meaning. Its expression remains instantly recognisable, yet even in general terms the definition of 'glam' remains unstable. Glam evades a fixed sense of chronology and timeframe with different meanings and connotations across national boundaries.

With its close proximity to popular culture and associations with kitsch and frivolity, glam is apparently beyond the framework of high-modernist and formalist ideology. Glam, though, can be interpreted through Charles Jencks' formulation of postmodernism as a term describing stylistic tendencies from the 1960s onwards. Broadly understood as a challenge to the rationalism of modernism, and applied by Jencks in relation to architecture, postmodernism was seen to prioritise eclecticism and pastiche over spontaneity and unique creative authenticity, effectively presupposing the collapse of modernist notions of progress. In this sense, postmodernism finds purchase with the stylistic eclecticism of glam, which combined a sense of revivalism and – crucially – futurity through its synthesis of visual iconography, from Marlene Dietrich to 1960s Pop art, Americana, high camp, and space-age chic.

Yet glam was more than a visual style and can more meaningfully be understood as an attitude or sensibility, its expression inseparable from its societal context. Glam also retains a powerful hold on the popular imagination and in contemporary style culture: nowadays glam seems to exist as a prism in the present, enabling us to view, refract and re-imagine artistic developments and cultural tendencies of the early 1970s.

At this time glam was the primary pop narrative. It offered a vision that conflated tantalisingly artificial glamour with dystopian futurity, mainlined to a mass audience in the form of the rock star as fictitious alien persona, or a series of real-life crimes seemingly inspired by the diabolic violence of Stanley Kubrick's *A Clockwork Orange* (which in 1973 led the director to withdraw the film from circulation in the United Kingdom).[1] Glam was British culture in acceleration, a social retuning brought about by manifestations as diverse as the costumed one-upmanship of Slade and the Sweet, whose

Opposite and above: Martin Parr
Osmonds Fans, Manchester 1973
Pigment prints on paper

John McManus
Roxette c.1977
16mm film, colour, sound
Duration: 15 minutes 58 seconds

Above: Bruce McLean
Pose Work for Plinths 1 1971
Photographs on board

Opposite: Patrick Procktor
Gervase 1968
Acrylic on canvas

absurd performances were disseminated *en masse* through the ritualised weekly viewing of *Top of the Pops*, through David Bowie's supposedly casual claim of being bisexual in 1972, through to Lindsay Kemp's 1975 theatrical production of *Flowers* at the Roundhouse Theatre in London, a piece based on Jean Genet's *Our Lady of the Flowers* (1943).

Glam rock, as Dave Hickey suggests, heralded the end zone of closeted male homosexuality, with the 'rhetoric of deniable disclosure' being appropriated by David Bowie and others. With glam, the language of theatrical transgression resonated throughout British society.[2] Considered in the context of manifestations such as Andrew Logan's omni-sexual Alternative Miss World pageant (which emerged in 1972), tendencies in post-1968 art identified in Jean-Christophe Ammann's 1974 exhibition *Transformer*[3] (which explored artists' 'capacity to visualize the masculine/feminine interface by means of ambivalent images'[4]) and the staged mediations of General Idea, glam rock was a phenomenon - played out at the leading-edge of popular culture - that brought about a heightened sense of self-awareness and self-identity. Glam proposed the possibility of self-reinvention and the assertion of marginal identity as a life choice, heralded by the body politic being made legible within an expanded politics of inclusion.

THE 'IN' CROWD
Always be smartly dressed, well groomed, relaxed, friendly, polite and in complete control. (*Gilbert & George*, Law of Sculptors)[5]

The role of the British art school of the late 1950s and 1960s in fermenting artistic and cultural experimentation contributed to the emergence of glam rock in 1971. As historian Robert Hewison notes, the art school at this time became 'a haven for imaginative people otherwise neglected by the educational system... the relative freedom of the art schools encouraged experiments with style. For working class students they were an escape from the factory, for middle class students they were the entry to bohemia.'[6] At this time Britain had more art schools per capita than any other country in the world. Their flexible recruitment policies contributed to a move away from class hierarchies and prejudices, producing a culture of bohemianism and ease against a backdrop of rising economic affluence and pop optimism. It was at British art schools – in London and across the provinces - that a generation of aspiring musicians converged, with ample time to rehearse.

Also emergent was a spirit of creative interdisciplinarity. This was expressed, for example, at the Royal

The Moodies – a group of art students who started to parody the current obsession with nostalgia, then found themselves being taken seriously

Report by *Meriel McCooey*; photographs by *Hans Feurer*

The Moodies
Sunday Times Magazine,
23 June 1974

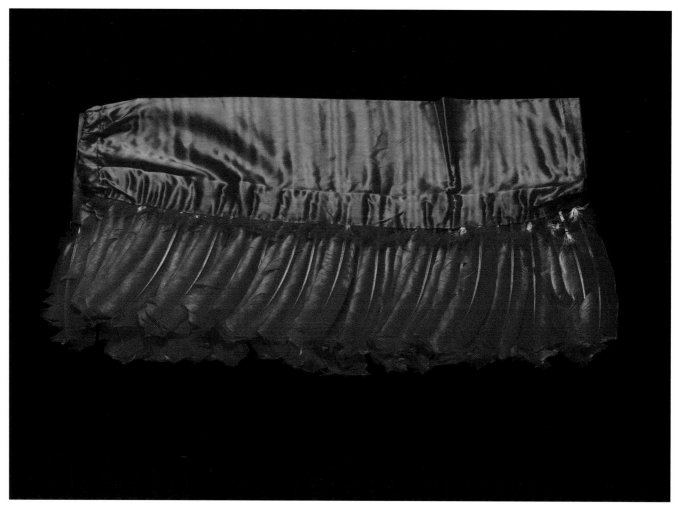

James Lee Byars
The Wings for Writing 1972
Silk, plumes

Asco (Glugio 'Gronk' Nicandro, Patssi Valdez, Willie Herron III, Harry Gamboa Jr.)
Walking Mural 1972
Digital print of colour photograph by Harry Gamboa Jr.

College of Art (a key art school of the emergence of a 'postmodern sensibility' in Britain) through its graphically forward-thinking journal *Ark*, which was an important expression of pop art, reflecting the sense of life and identity being increasingly visualised through the world of modern consumer culture, television and through mass mediation.[7]

Art students' openness to the relevance of all creative experience led to a promiscuous intermingling of ideas and ideals across the disciplines of fashion, design and applied arts, fine art and pop music. Richard Hamilton's *Swingeing London 67 (f)* 1968-9 is emblematic of this coming together, through its appropriation of a mediated image of the gallerist Robert Fraser handcuffed to Mick Jagger following their appearance in court on drugs charges. The era's liberal art-informed ambience also fuelled the imagination of David Bowie, who followed a curriculum infused with art and graphic design at Bromley Technical College. In 1969 Bowie also co-founded the Beckenham Arts Lab, a centre hosting artists' studios, poetry readings, light shows and theatrical and dance performances.

The art school was vital to the surfacing of Roxy Music as a fully formed *objet d'art* in 1972. A central narrative in this regard is Richard Hamilton's influence while teaching at the King Edward VII School of Art, University of Durham. There he taught, among others, Bryan Ferry, leader and 'author of Roxy Music... as an idea, and as a specific musical and imagistic concept.'[8] Following Hamilton's teachings, Roxy Music became 'above all else, a state of mind.'[9] Hamilton later created an extended series of works (1969-73) deploying cosmetic make-up as pigment, sometimes glitter, and collaging images drawn from high-end fashion magazines that, like glam, presented identity and idealised notions of glamour as an artificial and aestheticised construct.

Towards the end of the 1960s the synthesis between art and lifestyle, traceable to the high 1960s mod culture, had evolved into a culture of refined dandyism, articulated in works such as David Hockney's portrait of Ossie Clark and Celia Birtwell *Mr and Mrs Clark and Percy* 1970-1. The work of Patrick Procktor can also be framed in the context of late 1960s dandyism. Procktor studied at the Slade in London from 1958 to 1962 and, as Ian Massey notes: '"performed" the role of an artist within a currency of self-constructed dandyism... [wearing] make-up in varying degrees of discretion: for Procktor there were the silver toenails, the eye shadow...'[10] In the spring of 1968 he met the 22-year old aspiring pop star and model Gervase Griffiths (who later that year modelled for Antony Price's Royal College of Art fashion degree show as well as for Mr. Fish, the designer of flamboyant clothes and 'man dresses' for the late 1960s and early

Asco (Glugio 'Gronk' Nicandro, Patssi Valdez, Willie Herron III,
Harry Gamboa Jr.)
The Gores 1974
Digital prints of colour photographs by Harry Gamboa Jr.

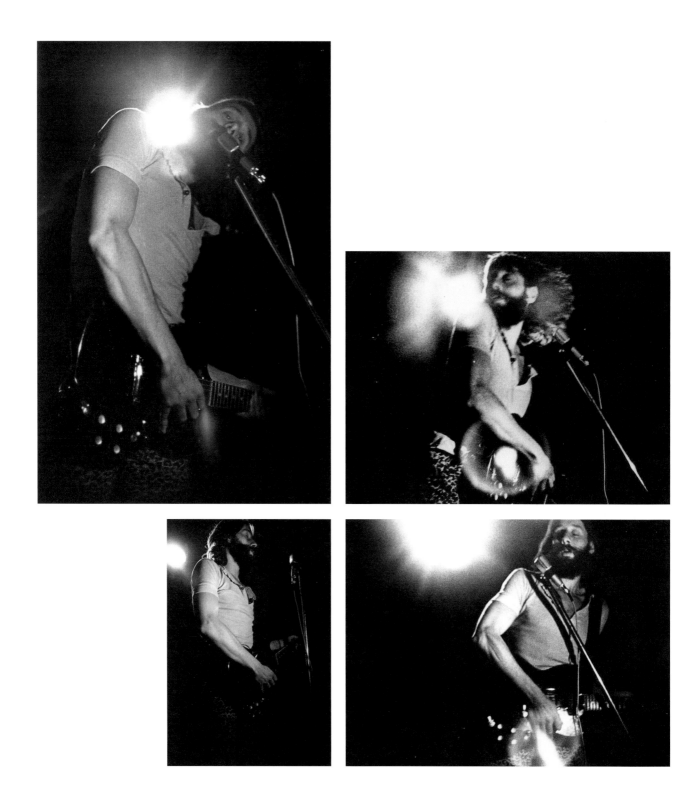

David Lamelas
Rock Star (Character Appropriation) 1974
Photographs mounted on aluminium

1970s pop glitterati.)[11] Procktor's series of paintings of Griffiths constitute heightened celebrations of male beauty, *Gervase* 1968 encapsulating the sun-kissed bloom of youth culture at the cusp of some revelatory transformation.

Jonathan Raban's 1974 book *Soft City* provides a perceptive insight into London's urban subconscious, portraying the city in a kind of post-1960s ennui, its most successful citizens being 'artists in surfaces, experts in self-preservation, adept stylists.'[12] Such expertise – the currency of the dandy – conveyed by the playing out of life as a kind of performance, a repertoire of learned gestures, manifest in the surface language of clothes and posture, or a list of 'cool' likes (and dislikes), epitomised the way in which personal style could come to subsume everyday reality.

In 1969 Gilbert & George designated themselves as 'living sculpture', creating performance works in which they wore matching dandyish suits and inscribed their names across their foreheads in glitter pigment.[13] In 1972 their video work *Portrait of the Artists as Young Men* offered an ultra-stylised pose of Gilbert & George as self-conscious aesthetes. Presented according to the artists' instructions with unnaturally high-contrast, the whited-out appearance of this video mirrors the exaggerated aesthetic polarity inherent in glam.

Gilbert & George's approach was shared by other artists who similarly recognised no distinction between their personae and their artistic production. James Lee Byars exemplified the use of dandyish pose as artistic tendency, creating art through gestures as ephemeral as kisses. His extravagantly refined clothing – gold lamé suits or red silk feathered winged sleeves – was integral to his art.

Like Gilbert & George, Bruce McLean and Paul Richards studied at St. Martin's School of Art in London during the 1960s. In 1971 they were co-founders of the Nice Style Pose Band, a collaborative performance group dedicated to the problems of performance and notions of the 'perfect' pose. The group's poses aimed to confront the pretensions of the art world whilst focusing on the role of body image and style characteristic of 1970s popular culture. In particular, their references to glam rock were in part motivated by their recognition of rock and roll's capacity for direct communication. As Nice Style member Gary Chitty notes: 'we were interested in glam rock and in having the best-shaped guitars... The whole visual imagery of rock music was inspiring to us, if not more inspiring than contemporary art at the time.'[14]

In a similar vein, performance groups such as Moody and the Menstruators (featuring artist Anne Bean and Polly Eltes, then partner of Roxy Music's publicist Simon Puxley)

Allen Jones
Chair 1969
Painted plastic and mixed media

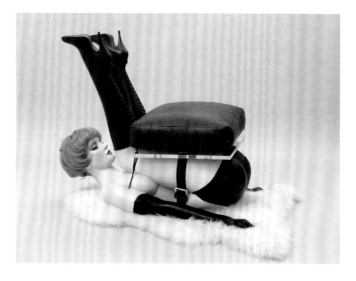

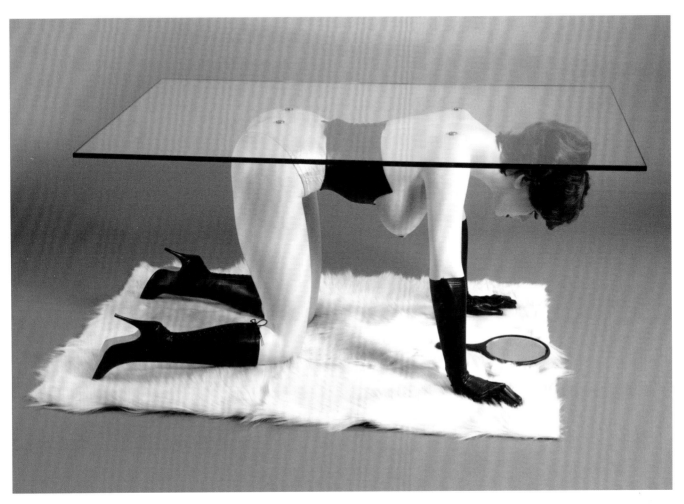

Allen Jones
Table 1969
Mixed media

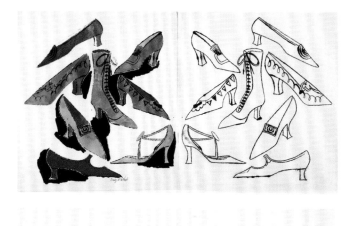

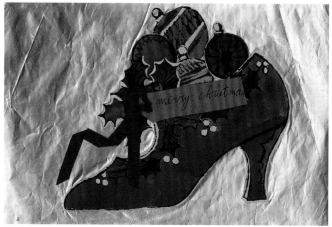

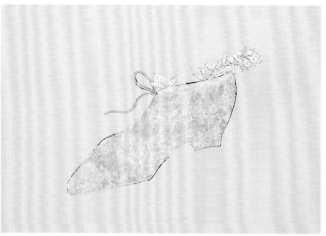

Left to right, top to bottom: Andy Warhol
Eight Shoes 1950s
Ink and Dr. Martin's Aniline dye on Strathmore paper

Merry Christmas Shoe c. 1957
Ink and Dr. Martin's Aniline dye on Strathmore and gold paper

Four Shoe Tips 1950s
Ink and graphite on Strathmore paper

High Heel with Shadow 1950s
Ink on Strathmore paper

Man's Shoe c. 1956
Gold leaf, ink, and stamped gold collage on Strathmore paper

Left to right, top to bottom: Andy Warhol
Screen Test: Nico 1966
Screen Test: Lou Reed (Coke) 1966
Screen Test: John Cale 1966
Screen Test: Sterling Morrison (Smoking), 1966
All 16mm film, black and white, silent, 4 minutes at 16fps

Mario Banana No. 1 1964
16mm film, colour, silent, 4 minutes at 16fps

deployed artifice, posing, concept and a flamboyant mode of retro glamour, exemplifying the conflation of a fine art sensibility and popular culture at this time. Tangential traces of glam can also be discerned in many of Derek Jarman's Super8 films of the 1970s, testifying to the sophisticated post-art school milieu in London inhabited by 'people who live their lives as an Art Experience in every possible way.'[15] As an exemplar, Jarman's *Duggie Fields at Home* 1974 constitutes a filmic essay manifest as a choreography of fixed camera positions, capturing Fields' artistic concern with pose and amplified personal style as a way of life.

THE GLAMOUR FACTORY

During the 1960s in the United States, idealised glamour was central to the emergence of the phenomenon of camp. At this time Jack Smith developed his artistic repertoire by appropriating the glamour archive of Hollywood, creating films and performances starring drag queens and transvestites who adopted the airs of the stars of yesteryear. Rejecting narrative concerns and seeking to override gender categorisations, in films such as *Flaming Creatures* 1963, Smith expresses the visual revelation available through faux and expansively trashy glamour that delights in its use of lowbrow high gloss effects. In Smith's hands Hollywood, once associated with the high-glamour staging of bodies and textures, is presented as a luridly ersatz lurid Hollywood, simultaneously celebratory homage and abject pastiche. As Susan Sontag points out, Smith's film *Flaming Creatures* is concerned with inter-sexuality; the 'primary image is the confusion of male and female flesh.'[16]

For Tom Holert, rather than being an aristocratic mode of expression emblematised by the performances of Marlene Dietrich, artists such as Smith deployed glamour to activate a more democratic and inclusive system of portrayal. His art anticipated the hyper-individualised states and gender inauthenticity inherent in glam, as well as its evocation of mythical and exotic technological trash utopias.[17]

Andy Warhol's unwavering interest in glamour, style and fashion was central to glam, which adopted the artist's compulsive fascination with surface and pose. Furthermore Warhol's explicitly commercial concerns and interest in developing a profile beyond the art world meant that by the mid-1960s his ideas and iconography had migrated into the realm of popular culture. The silvering of the Factory walls by Billy Name in 1964 to create an environment of reflective surfaces - perfect for pose and narcissistic performance as perpetual modus operandi - constitutes one of the key conceptual foundations for glam.[18] As Pat Hackett notes: 'it was a perfect time to think silver.

Opposite: Derek Jarman
Miss Gaby - I'm Ready for My Close-Up 1972
Super8 film, colour
Duration: 6 minutes

Above: Derek Jarman
Duggie Fields at Home 1974
Super8 film, colour
Duration: 2 minutes

Nice Style
Pre-Performance Pose at Sonia Henie Niels Onstad Foundation, Oslo 1972
Photographs, colour, on paper

Silver was the future, it was spacey – the astronauts wore silver suits... and their equipment was silver, too. And silver was also the past – the Silver Screen – Hollywood actresses photographed in silver sets. And maybe more than anything, silver was narcissism – mirrors were backed with silver.'[19]

Warhol understood pop's fundamental communicability and its capacity to project and inculcate a particular state of mind. Through the white heat of the 1960s, Warhol conjured a parallel universe of glamour that anticipated the absurd posturing of glam, revelling in transgressive and ersatz sensation. In advance of the cosmetic spectacle of glam, Warhol posited that anybody could be elevated to superstar status through strategies of self-staging, and a number of his superstars have roles in the genealogy of glam: Cyrinda Foxe appears in the Mick Rock directed promotional film for David Bowie's 'Jean Genie' (1973) while Eric Emerson fronted the Magic Tramps. Critically, the decadent cool of the Velvet Underground provided a central reference point for both Roxy Music and David Bowie, the latter re-formulating the Warhol screen test for his promotional video for 'Life on Mars' (1972). Transvestites Candy Darling, Jackie Curtis and Holly Woodlawn were mainstays at the Factory, celebrated in Lou Reed's 'Walk on the Wild Side' (1972). The drag culture in New York was powerfully captured in the photography of Peter Hujar, with Nan Goldin's earliest photographs similarly offering a portal into
a parallel realm of glamour. As Warhol pointed out in 1975: 'when they took the movie stars and stuck them in the kitchen, they weren't stars any more – they were just like you and me. Drag queens are reminders that some stars still aren't just like you or me.'[20]

Warhol also influenced the conceptual development of Roxy Music. Warhol superstar Baby Jane Holzer was name-checked in the lyrics of Roxy Music's first single 'Virginia Plain' (its title referring to a painting created by Bryan Ferry while under the tutelage of Richard Hamilton). Ferry's fellow student Mark Lancaster provides another link between Warhol and glam, spending time at the Factory (at Hamilton's suggestion) where he met Jack Smith and starred in Warhol's film *Kiss* (1964). Bowie's invention of multiple fictional personae through the 1970s might be understood as Warholian. In 1971 Bowie, channelling Warhol, declared: 'I'm just picking up on what other people say... I'm not thinking for myself anymore... I'd rather take the position of being a Photostat machine with an image'.[21] In May 1971 the Warhol-produced play *Pork* opened in New York. In July it transferred to the Roundhouse in London, where the cast were photographed during rehearsals by the

artist Billy Sullivan (who was engaged as the set-designer for the performance). While in London the cast also met with Bowie, who recruited them *en masse* to staff Mainman, his first management company in the United States.[22]

TRANSFORMER

If we are all members of one body, then in that one body there is neither male nor female; or rather there is both: it is an androgynous or hermaphroditic body, containing both sexes [...] The division of the one man into two sexes is part of [our] fall.'[23]
(Norman O. Brown, in Love's Body, 1966)

Kids are finding out that there isn't much difference between them sexually. They are finding out that the sexual terms homosexual, bisexual, heterosexual, all those are just words in front of sexual. People are just sexual.' (David Johansen, The New York Dolls, 1973)

Glam constituted a late flowering of psychedelic culture and a continuation of currents that emerged within the radical counter-culture of the 1960s (in fact, key glam figures such as David Bowie and Marc Bolan were both invested in the era's hippie culture and style.) As Mike Kelley notes, the anti-Vietnam War movement of the late 1960s and early 1970s was characterised by overt demonstrations of femininity and male homosexuality as an expression of resistance and a means to escape the draft, which for Kelley constituted the root of the feminine posturing which found its apex with 1970s glam rock.[24]

The shift towards a diffused notion of gender – and the use of gender play, masquerade and artistic self-staging – was a conspicuous art narrative at this time. It was a shift also played out in pop culture through manifestations as diverse as the Byron-esque visage of Mick Jagger at the Rolling Stones Hyde Park concert of 1969 (the figure of the androgynous rock star embodying the assumed liberation of roles and abolition of borders between sexual identities) through to the era's penchant for the costumes of traditional Japanese theatre, the 'noh' mask as an impassive performance of gender with men playing women's roles and vice-versa, reflected also in the fashion photography of the period and in David Bowie's commissioning of Kansai Yamamoto to create his stage costumes.[25] Androgyny was also evident in Rudi Gernreich's 'unisex' fashion collection of 1969, which the designer lifted from Adam the Second (the Late Paul Cotton), an artist whose complex performative practice explored ideas of self-mythology through his professed embodiment of the meta-Freudian theories of Norman O. Brown. Brown claimed a radical potential within the very corporeal body of mankind,

proposing that the very comprehension of life lay in the differences between entities - a radical concept of indeterminacy enacted by both genders being present within a single body.

Within this context we can also regard the work of Jürgen Klauke and Ulay. Klauke's work was informed by the writings and philosophies of George Bataille, who believed that the extremes of human behaviour could reveal to mankind the absolute truths of existence. In photo-works such as *Transformer* 1973, Klauke's appearance reflected the full-tilt glam look of the era: an attempt by the artist to occupy both male and female roles, manifest through his use of quasi-alien androgyny, pancake make-up, with the artist wearing red leather platform boots with female sex organs and penis nipple appendages. Similar concerns are evident in Ulay's auto-Polaroid works of the early 1970s, the artist problematising the notion of binary gender definitions.

A wider examination of art and performance of the early 1970s reveals shared concerns between artists and artist collectives in Britain, Europe and in United States. In Detroit, for example, the birthplace of the proto-glam rock group the MC5 and Iggy and the Stooges, there emerged Destroy All Monsters, an art-rock collective whose membership included Mike Kelley, Jim Shaw, Cary Loren and Niagara. Destroy All Monsters expressed a form of postmodern aesthetic delirium and had wildly diverse influences, embracing the trash aesthetics of Jack Smith, John Waters, the Velvet Underground, William Burroughs, Krautrock, the Hairy Who and the White Panthers. The use of appropriation as an artistic strategy was also integral to the work of Jack Goldstein. In *The Jump* of 1978, Goldstein offers a patina of 1970s visuality by presenting a man made out of stars performing a somersault and disappearing from the frame of the projected image, isolating and presenting a looped iteration of a transient spectacle typically associated with the surface effects of Hollywood.

Such collective practice and critical engagement with popular culture can also be traced to artist groups such as General Idea, as well as to Asco, a collective that emerged out of the Chicano culture of Los Angeles. As Amelia Jones points out, rather than deploying affirmative expressions of marginal identity – ideas played out in key gender and identity debates of the 1970s – Asco's agenda was wider and explored both affirmative and also critical notions of mainstream cultural ideology.[26] In the *Gores* series, Asco – donning extravagant glam-rock styled outfits - staged themselves in film-stills for non-existent movies, creating highly ambiguous documents that exist somewhere between concept art and performance

Katherina Sieverding
Transformer 1973/74
Video projection, colour, silent

Aubrey Beardsley

An exhibition of original drawings, manuscripts, books, paintings, posters etc.

at The Victoria and Albert Museum

From 19th May to 19th September 1966

Poster for Aubrey Beardsley exhibition at the Victoria and Albert Museum, London 1966
Colour offset lithograph

Opposite: *Poster for the New York Dolls, live at Biba, London* 1973
Printed poster

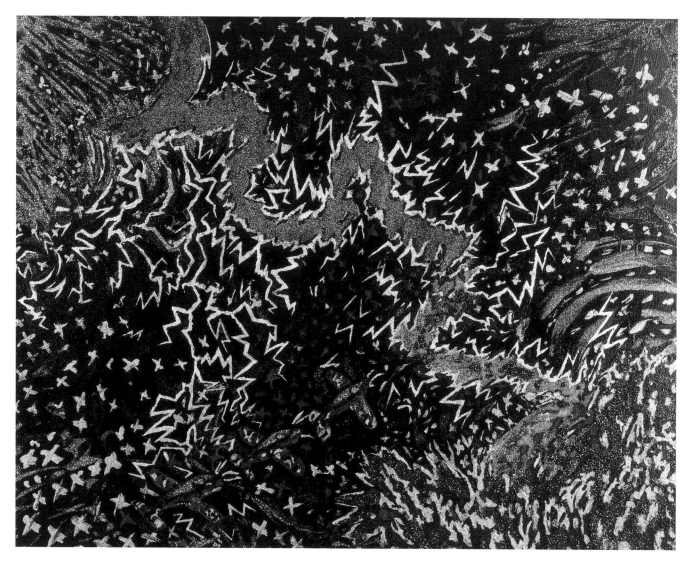

Robert Malaval
In the Storm (Three Small Planes) 1975
Acrylic and glitter on canvas

documentation. The works affirm their identity as Chicanos, whilst simultaneously drawing attention to their invisibility within the context of the Hollywood movie industry that provided a context for their artistic practice. The artistic use of self-staging and auto-transformation can be extended to the pioneering works of Cindy Sherman and Eleanor Antin, through to works such as David Lamela's *Rock Star (Character Appropriation)* 1974.

An examination of 1970s art, performance and style reveals a sense of morphic resonance across geographical boundaries. Such pooling of influence – sometimes enabled by mail-art strategies or collaborative practice – show the myriad ways in which artistic and style innovations such as glam traversed art, magazines, social engagement, and the popular media. By linking a diversity of artistic concerns of the period, such as the fascination with the power and processes of the media, it becomes possible to rethink 1970s art and style. It reveals how glam constituted a migration of fine art ideas and approaches to the front-line of popular culture, whose expression continues to permeate our contemporary imagination.

2 Dave Hickey, 'A Rhinestone as Big as the Ritz', *Air Guitar: Essays on Art and Democracy*, Los Angeles, California: Art Issues, 1997, p. 59.

3 *Transformer* was staged at the Kunstmuseum Luzern from 17 March to 4 April 1974, touring to the Neue Galerie Am Landesmuseum Joanneau, Graz, and Museum Bochum, and explored the explored ideas of gender ambiguity in art in the context of post-1968 popular culture.

4 Cited in Claude-Hubert Tatot et al, *Who the Hell is Herman, Anyway?*, Genève, Quiquandquoi, 2003, p. 34.

5 Cited in Carter Ratcliff, 'Gilbert & George and modern life', in *Gilbert & George: The Complete Pictures, 1971-1985*, New York, Rizzoli, 1986, p. 7.

6 Robert Hewison, *Too Much: Art and Society in the Sixties, 1960– 75* London: Methuen, 1986, pp. 63–64.

7 See Alex Seago, *Burning the Box of Beautiful Things: The Development of a Postmodern Sensibility*, Oxford: Clarendon, 1995.

8 Michael Bracewell, *Remake/Remodel: Art, Pop, Fashion and the Making of Roxy Music*, London: Faber and Faber, 2007, p. 6.

9 ibid., p. 4.

10 Cited in Ian Massey, *Patrick Procktor: Art and Life*, London: Unicorn Press, 2010, p. 120.

11 See, for example, David Bowie wearing Pre-Raphaelite dress on the LP cover for *The Man Who Sold the World* 1971.

12 Raban writes: 'to be part of the city, you needed a city style – an economic grammar of identity through which you could project yourself. Clearly, this was something to be learned, an expertise […] If you could not get the surface right, what hope was there of expressing whatever lay beneath it?' In *Soft City*, London: Hamish Hamilton, 1974, p. 54.

13 Anne Rorimer, *Photography: Restructuring the Pictorial, New Art in the 60s and 70s*, London: Thames & Hudson, 2004 (resvd.), p. 143. At this time the artists also performed *Posing Piece* 1969, in which they stood silent on the staircase of the Stedelijk Museum in Amsterdam, again in their trademark suits and metal face made-up.

14 See 'Nice Style: The World's First Pose Band: Gary Chitty, Bruce McLean and Paul Richards in conversation with Jon Wood', http://www.henry-moore.org/docs/file_1324400255468_0.pdf (accessed 4 January 2012).

15 Peter York, 'Style Wars', *AA Files*, No. 1 (Winter 1981–82), p. 27.

16 Susan Sontag, 'Jack Smith's "Flaming Creatures"', in *The New American Cinema: A Critical Anthology*, Gregory Battcock, ed., New York: E. P. Dutton, 1967, pp. 208–210.

17 Smith's performances are played out on extravagant stage sets meticulously constructed from the accumulated trash of modern civilisation - bottles, old Christmas trees and broken toys. Jonas Mekas likened Smith's performances to the end of civilisation 'which it seemed to portray […] this set became like this culture that seems to absorb everything and everybody…' Cited in 'Jack Smith, or the End of Civilisation', in *Jack Smith: Flaming Creature: His Amazing Life and Times*, London and New York: Serpent's Tail, pp. 48–49.

18 Mark Francis and Margery King, "The Warhol Look", in *The Warhol Look*, Pittsburgh: The Andy Warhol Foundation, 1999, p. 23.

19 Andy Warhol and Pat Hackett, *POPism: The Warhol Sixties*, New York: Harcourt Brace Jovanovich, 1980, pp. 64–65.

20 Andy Warhol, *From A to B and Back Again: The Philosophy of Andy Warhol*, New York: Harcourt Brace Jovanovich, 1975, pp. 54–55.

21 Peter Doggett: *The Man Who Sold the World: David Bowie and the 1970s*, London: Bodley Head, 2011, pp. 120–121.

22 The star and transvestite cast member Jayne County would later claim that Bowie was 'studying our make-up for his own future use. His whole look came from us.', in ibid., p. 122.

23 Norman O. Brown, 'Unity', in *Love's Body*, New York: Random House, 1966, p. 84.

24 Mike Kelley, 'Cross Gender/Cross Genre', *Performance Art Journal* 64, The John Hopkins University Press, p. 2.

25 On this see Roland Barthes, 'The Written Face', Sandy MacDonald (trans.), *The Drama Review*, Vol. 15, No. 2, (Spring, 1971), pp. 80–82.

26 Amelia Jones, 'Traitor Prophets: Asco's Art as Politics of the In-Between', *ASCO: Elite of the Obscure* (exh. cat.), Los Angeles County Museum of Art pp. 108–9.

1 See for example '"Clockwork Orange" link with boy's crime', reporting a teenager's conviction for murdering a sixty-year old vagrant in an apparent copycat crime. In the *The Times*, 4 July 1973.

For Your Pleasure: The Quest for Glamour in British Fashion 1969–1972

Judith Watt

Antony Price, more 'image-maker' than fashion designer, had a significant impact on the glamourous music world of 1970s London.[1] When he arrived as a 20-year-old at the Royal College of Art's Fashion Design School in 1965 it was a creative hub, transforming its postgraduate students into influential young British fashion designers, a new phenomenon of the post-war era. 'No-one knew what I was talking about when I said I wanted to be one,' remembers Sheilagh Brown, who graduated from the school in 1969. 'They'd say "fashion designer – what's that?" But the Royal College was special at that particular point in time. It was *glamorous*; the number one college for glamour. Because David Hockney and Ossie Clark had been there, it epitomised everything about the 1960s – young, creative design that was about lifestyle as well as fashion. It was the glossy side of art school'.[2]

Karl Stoecker
Antony Price 1972
C-type crystal archive print on paper

39

Hockney, who graduated from the painting school of the Royal College in 1962, described a freshness in the early 1960s: 'You didn't let the commercial side interfere with things, in film, music, painting, fashion. It was an energy driven by the bohemian world'.[3] Malcolm Bird, who would later become cutter, designer and illustrator at Biba, recalls seeing the name of Ossie Clark, another notable graduate, on a locker at his Royal College interview in 1965. Clark's significance was enhanced by appearing in *Vogue*'s August 1965 issue as one of the new faces in fashion, underlining the Royal College's position in producing talented fashion designers; alumnae Marion Foale and Sally Tuffin sold 'Pop' mini-dresses and trouser suits at their shop off Carnaby Street, Clark's clothes were sold at Woollands 21 and Quorum and Sylvia Ayton's paper dresses with Pop prints by Zandra Rhodes were hot sellers at Miss Selfridge.

Bird, Clark and Price were part of an influx from the north that infiltrated the fashion department at the Royal College, hitherto dominated by students from the Greater London area. Like Clark, who had studied fashion at Manchester College of Art, Price had developed cutting skills in the more traditional, technical-based fashion diploma course at Bradford College of Art. Both combined technical ability with the acute visual sensibilities and love of exhibitionism that were the foundations of the 'glam' aesthetic. The potential of unique personal style – a pose – was essential. Price first found it in Janey Ironside, the first Professor of Fashion at the Royal College (1956–1968): 'All we cared about was what she looked like,' he says. 'She was inspirational'.[4] Under her aegis the diploma course became a factory for a generation of designers such as Sheilagh Brown, Rose Bradford, Freddie Burretti, Ossie Clark, Jim O'Connor, Pamela Motown, Barbara Hulanicki, Lloyd Johnson, Antony Price and Jane Whiteside.

In her 1968 book *A Fashion Alphabet*, Ironside wrote: 'Fashion in clothing is one of the great living arts of civilisation. Fashion is contemporary life on a personal scale'.[5] Her aim with the Royal College fashion course was to develop an 'internationally accepted new English look', regarding fashion as an integral part of culture.[6] She achieved this partly by giving confidence to her most ambitious students. Price recalled, 'We didn't want to be couturiers. We assumed that we would take them all to the cleaners and wipe the floor with them. We were about the street. Anything Establishment had to be challenged'.[7] The most avant-garde Royal College students were not particulary interested in high fashion and couture, instead styling themselves after films such as Federico Fellini's *Juliet of the Spirits* (1965) or William Klein's *Qui êtes-vous, Polly Maggoo?* (1966), before going out clubbing at Le Kilt and the Bag of Nails.

West One, 8 February 1974
(With Marc Bolan on cover)

Tim Street-Porter
Pop art food hall at Biba 1973

David Hockney
Mr and Mrs Clark and Percy 1970-1
Acrylic on canvas

Top: Ossie Clark
Fantasy design woman wearing a black suit with bustier and coq feathers at the shoulders 1974
Ink on paper

Left: 'Glamamoto!', British *Vogue*, October 1971

Opposite: Karl Stoecker
Sparks – Kimono my House (variant) 1974
C-type crystal archive print on paper

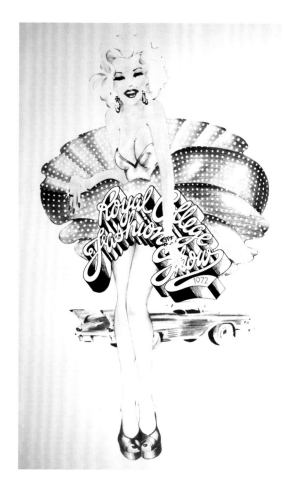

Left to right, top to bottom:
Royal College of Art Fashion Degree Show Catalogue 1972

Malcolm Bird
Calender (Girl Holding King Kong) 1972

Royal College of Art Fashion Degree Show Catalogue 1968

Opposite, top: 'Mr. Freedom feature', *Nova*, May 1970

Opposite, below: 'Mickey ist Verstört (Mr. Freedom feature)',
Twen magazine, September 1971

Mickey ist versäbt

Karl Stoecker
Brian Eno wearing stage costume designed by Carol McNicoll 1973
C-type crystal archive print on paper

Opposite: Karl Stoecker
Bryan Ferry wearing stage costume designed by Antony Price 1973
C-type crystal archive print on paper

By 1967 an interest had emerged in the retro glamour of Art Deco. At the Royal College Professor Bernard Nevill introduced students to the fashion illustration of the inter-war period, such as that of Erté, the designers Vionnet and Schiaparelli, and Hollywood's silver screen. Also of influence were films such as the Busby Berkeley-choreographed *Footlight Parade* (1933) and *I'm No Angel* (1933) featuring Mae West, images shimmering with a brittle brilliance. Clark was the first to reflect this influence in his degree collection, showing his Robert Indiana Op-art print coat with looks inspired by 1930s movie stars. 'The whole glamour thing of the 1930s was what influenced us,' Clark later acknowledged. 'We thought, "Why can't people in the street wear them?"'[8] In 1967 Clark launched his maxi-coat and bias-cut dresses with prints by Celia Birtwell. His designs were the opposite of the iconic Pop mini-skirt, and hit the new mood. 'Anything to do with our parents' awful 1950s taste was what we hated,' says Price. 'Biba was fantastic, introducing "granny" colours, sludgy purples and blues, dropping hemlines, making women look like '20s and '30s femmes fatales.'[9] The aesthetic filtering through the imaginations of designers in the late 1960s was above all *cinematic*.

The Electric on Portobello Road was the cinema of choice for the Ladbroke Grove 'in-crowd', which included art director Brian Morris, David Hockney and Peter Schlesinger, Eric Boman, sculptor Mo McDermott, Ossie Clark, Celia Birtwell, Jane Whiteside, Sheilagh Brown, Antony Price and his girlfriend Juliet Mann. With the air wreathed in grass smoke they watched Marlene Dietrich in von Sternberg's *The Devil is a Woman* (1935), Fred Astaire in *Flying Down to Rio* (1933) and Mae West in anything. In April 1970, when Biba launched a cosmetics range for the Dorothy Perkins chain, Malcolm Bird designed a cake for the event with the figure of Mae West reclining on a bed of red marzipan roses.[10] For Price, Max Reinhardt's *A Midsummer Night's Dream* (1935) was particularly influential. Shot with tungsten lighting, filmed through layers of sparkling gauze, Victor Jory's horned costume for the character of Oberon evoked the glamour and twinkling aura that Price sought to achieve with the green and black sequinned jacket worn by Bryan Ferry for his first appearance on *Top of the Pops* in August 1972. The camp of it all, the artifice and exaggeration, translated in the early 1970s from film costume onto the street.

Price had joined Jane Whiteside as menswear designer at Stirling Cooper in 1968; a year later it opened its first shop in Wigmore Street, London, an extraordinary oriental interior with a dragon's mouth framing the door. While at Stirling Cooper, Price's own look was remarkable. Each venture outside his home was a performance, based on a desire not only to improve but to exaggerate the way he looked. He aimed for 'savage and fantastic', a snake-boy with glitter eyeshadow, false eyelashes, ersatz freckles, and black hair extensions streaked with silver. His six-foot frame was raised by four-inch heeled platform shoes and, clad in a sequinned tiger-print jacket and black leather trousers, he became a latter-day realisation of Charles Baudelaire's dandy-hero, with a 'burning desire to create a personal form of originality... a cult of the ego... the pleasure of causing surprise in others, and the proud satisfaction of never showing any oneself'.[11]

The first customers at Stirling Cooper were the Rolling Stones. Price's menswear was new in combining a 'straight' Clark Gable silhouette with a gay sensibility. He was influenced by the artwork of Tom of Finland, a graphic paradise of long-torsoed, small-waisted, broad-shouldered and big-packaged supermen at a time when, according to Sir Paul Smith, most men were wearing 'navy or grey suits'.[12] Price's innovation was to reshape the male body through cutting and tailoring, to redefine the masculine silhouette, reacting against a unisex trend of narrow hips and flat chests. His 'bridge crotch' trousers of 1969 completed the look. Lloyd Johnson of Cockell and Johnson, the style-setting boutique in Kensington Market, described the effect succinctly: 'What they did was to push your goolies forward from the back then push your cock up at the front and lift your buttocks up at the back.'[13] A series of Price's fitted stretch cap-sleeved T-shirts with camp motifs were selling at the rate of a million a year under the Plaza label, modelled in one shoot by Amanda Lear and Eric Boman, and David Bowie wore an adaptation of the bridge-crotch trousers in the telephone box scene for the *Ziggy Stardust* album in 1972.[14]

Styled by Chelita Secunda, a former PR of Ossie Clark's, Marc Bolan had worn glitter for his performance of 'Hot Love' on *Top of the Pops* on 10 March 1971, creating a seminal moment in the history of glam style. Yet Bolan had been dressing in Tolkien-drag the year before and for some his style was too much like fancy dress. 'Bolan was too straight and he wasn't part of the Ladbroke Grove scene', says Price, who dismissed him because he didn't 'live' the style.[15] This contrasted with figures such as Lloyd Johnson, who described himself, Price and Freddie Burretti, who made clothes for Bowie, as integrally 'style people'. In fact, they were style leaders, their personal vision essentially transgressive and their work beyond the comprehension of the conventional fashion press, which in general was not aligned with the gay and bisexual in-crowd, the ex-art school scene that defined the new fashion designers and musicians. The most popular place to go at night was the gay club Yours and Mine on Kensington High Street. 'Everybody who was a Face or hip went to the club; Ossie, Eric, Peter Hinwood, Lloyd, Derek Jarman and Andrew Logan', says Price.[16] The women central to the scene, such as model Gala

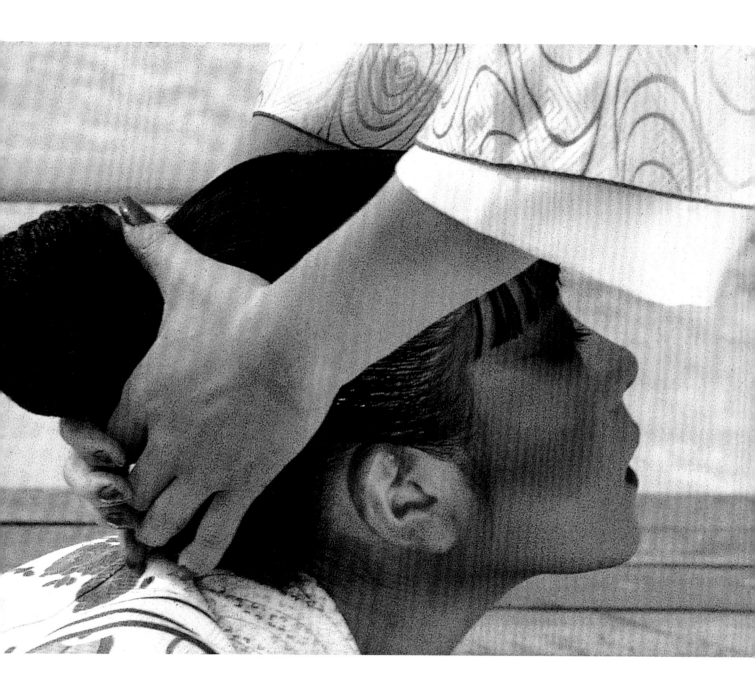

Guy Bourdin
Fashion Film (Geisha Girls) 1974
Super8 film, colour, sound
Duration: 1 minute 7 seconds

Mitchell, Jane Whiteside, Amanda Lear and Juliet Mann, looked like glamourous 1940s Hollywood femmes fatales, experimenting with personal style and changing themselves drastically from one week to the next.

The trend for glamour became a story with Ken Russell's *The Boyfriend* (1971) in the cinemas. Price, collaborating with photographer Karl Stoecker and make-up artist Pierre Laroche in early 1971, had pushed the limits of fashion with a series of 'test' pictures featuring Amanda Lear and Gala, a prequel to the sexual subversion of *The Rocky Horror Show* (1973) and the drama of Bowie's maquillaged image on the cover of *Aladdin Sane*, both of which featured Laroche's work. As Johnson noted, 'Bowie brought together all these elements and packaged them'.[17]

In spring 1971, Dave Shimeld, owner of Che Guevara, held an Ossie Clark fashion show in Kingly Street with Price as the warm-up. It provided a platform for Price's innovative, tongue-in-cheek 1950s styles, and it was here that he first met and worked with Clark's models Kari-Ann Muller and Gala Mitchell. 'I fell for Gala hook line and sinker after seeing her in action,' says Price. 'She was as camp as a row of tents, the toast of gay London'.[18] One of the people in the audience was Bryan Ferry. Price's ideas were newer, closest to his; the clothes sculpted the body, and Price's idea of 'glamour' – working with a 1950s sexuality and a visceral contemporary energy – was what Ferry wanted to capture on Roxy Music's first album cover.

There was also *Vogue*'s feature, 'GLAMAMOTO', in October 1971 showcasing the Japanese designer Kansai Yamamoto's 'extraordinary evening clothes, pure theatre'.[19] Challenging the traditional Western silhouette, Yamamoto went on to provide kabuki-based designs for David Bowie's Ziggy Stardust and Aladdin Sane personae. The collaboration between Gala, Price and Stoecker continued in 1972 when Stoecker photographed Gala in his Paddington studio, styled by Price and wearing his ciré satin bodice designed for the boutique Che Guevara, for the back of Lou Reed's album *Transformer*.

In the spring of 1972 Ferry asked the designer if he would like to work with him to produce the album's cover and inside images. In Price's words, not only did Ferry get a designer, but he got a model (Kari-Ann), photographer (Karl Stoecker), hair stylist (Keith Wainwright at Smile) and clothes too. Price recalls, 'Bryan came round to my flat with a picture of Rita Hayworth in *Gilda*, wearing the white batwing top and split skirt. And I said "Of course! Hayworth as Gilda!" I was into the theatre of image and Bryan had this strange voice, writing weird wonderful songs like "Ladytron"; it was about the right look to go with the music and we were obsessed with images of perfection, old Hollywood

achieved through lighting, costume and sets made into the shape of things to come'.[20] Kari-Ann was styled by Price in homage to *Gilda*:[21] the boned top, shorts and wrap were part of his collection at Che Guevara, and the red peep-toe platform shoes he designed were made for him by Terry de Havilland. The band brought their own clothes, although Price had brought along a selection of his own clothes and menswear samples, 'just in case'. The contact sheets from the shoot no longer exist, but they would have revealed a Roxy Music line-up – Ferry, Eno, Andy McKay, Phil Manzanera, Graham Simpson and Paul Thompson – at first 'looking like normal jeans-wearing young men. After that, Bryan said "OK let's give it a go"'. Price pulled out what he had brought and the transformation began. As Ferry explained to the *Guardian*, 'We couldn't go on stage without some form of presentation. We don't associate sincerity in music with drabness in appearance'.[22]

By the time Bowie's LP *Aladdin Sane* came out in April 1973, Price and Roxy Music had moved on from glitter to something more visually interesting with *For Your Pleasure*: the *haute* fetish of black leather, a femme fatale leading a black panther like an urban bacchante. By April 1974 the finesse of 'glamour' had become a travesty. Gary Glitter informed the *NME* that 'Glamour is what I deal in… the Hollywood thing.' Price riposted: 'All that glitter crap is so grotesque… It's all dead and there aren't even any decent clubs for them to show the extent of their decay'.[23]

Opposite: Karl Stoecker
Polka Dot Pin-Up c.1972-3
C-type crystal archive print on paper

Right: Karl Stoecker with Allen Jones
Amanda Lear (Siren) c.1972-3
C-type crystal archive print on paper

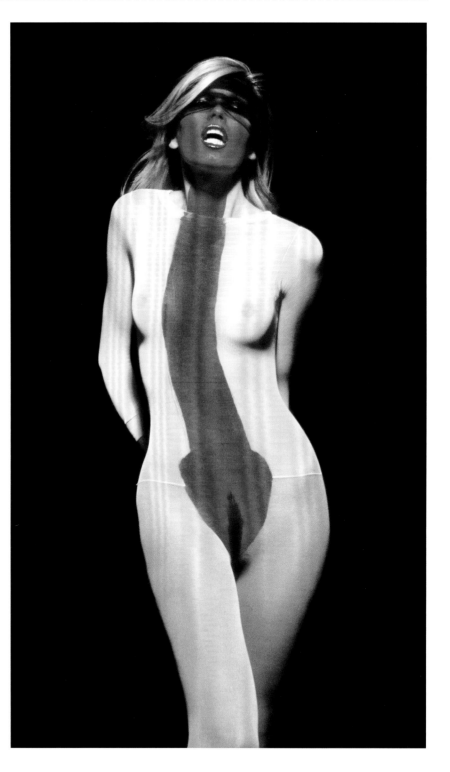

1 See Peter York, 'Them', *Harpers and Queen*, October 1976. 'Them' referred to the group of London-based people, intrinsic to the evolution and identity of 'glam' in the late 1960s and early 1970s, for whom artifice, immaculate presentation, visual wit and style were a reaction against the 'straight' world of unkempt hippies and the risible earnestness of prog-rock. Their aesthetic manifested itself as pure Beau Brummell dandyism via art school, identified by York as 'the art school bulge and the assimilation of camp'. See also Michael Bracewell, *Remake/Remodel: Art, Pop, Fashion and the Making of Roxy Music*, 1953–1972, London: Faber & Faber, 2007, p. 56.
2 Sheilagh Brown studied fashion design at the Royal College from 1966 to 1969. Interview with the author, 2012.
3 David Hockney, interview with the author, 2003, in *Judith Watt, Ossie Clark 1965–1974*, London: V&A Publications, 2003, p. 32.
4 Antony Price, interview with the author, 2012.
5 Janey Ironside, *A Fashion Alphabet*, London: Michael Joseph, 1968, p. 8.
6 Bracewell, *Remake/Remodel*, p. 287, quoting Virginia Ironside, *Janey and Me: Growing Up with My Mother*, London: Fourth Estate, 2003.
7 Price, interview with the author, 2012.
8 Watt, *Ossie Clark 1965–1974*, p. 39.
9 Price, interview with the author, 2012.
10 Alwyn W. Turner, *Biba: The Biba Experience*, London: Antique Collectors' Club, 2004, p. 41.
11 Charles Baudelaire, 'The Dandy', in *The Painter of Modern Life* (1863), from *Selected Writings on Art and Literature*, trans. P. E. Charvet, London: Viking, 1972.
12 Paul Smith, interview with the author, 1989.
13 Lloyd Johnson, interview with the author, 2012.
14 Price, interview with the author, 2012.
15 Ibid.
16 Ibid.
17 Johnson, interview with the author, 2012.
18 Price, interview with the author, 2012.
19 'And Now for the Amazing Mr Kansai Yamamoto', British *Vogue*, July 1971, pp. 102–3; and 'GLAMAMOTO: Satin and Brocade for Dressing Up Nights', British *Vogue*, October 1971, pp. 118–19.
20 Ibid.
21 *Gilda* (1946), directed by Charles Vidor, costumes designed by Jean Louis.
22 Robin Denselow, 'Roxy... a new phenomenon in rock music', *The Guardian*, October 1972, cited in Bracewell, *Remake/Remodel* p. VI – VII.
23 Nick Kent, 'The Politics of Flash', *New Musical Express*, 6 April 1974, with thanks to Paul Gorman, The Look, www.rockandpopfashion.com.

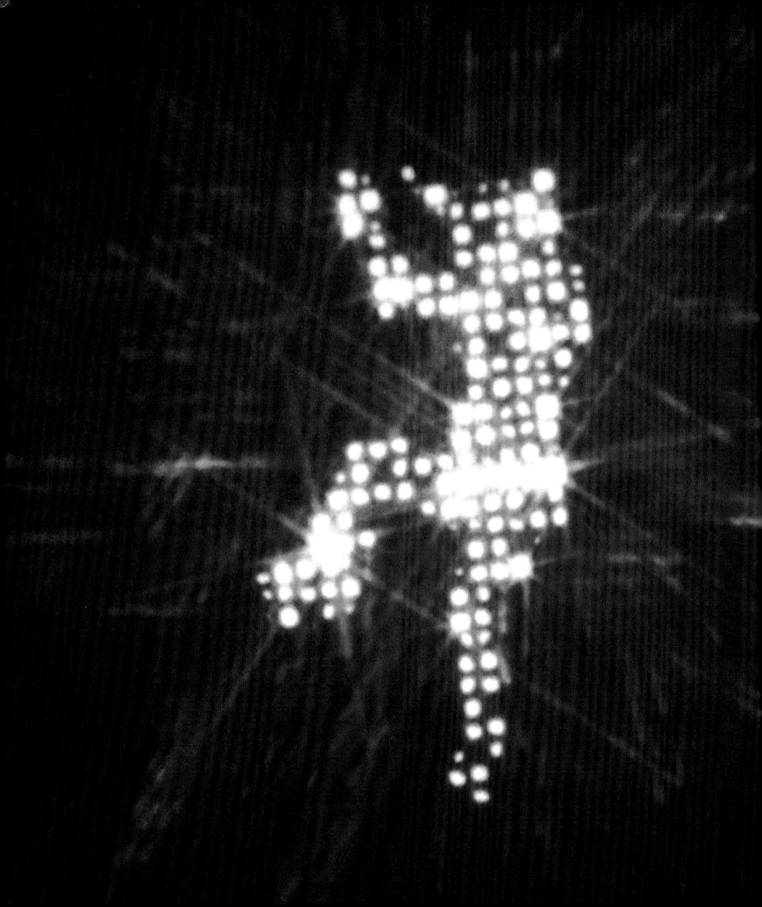

Cross Gender/Cross Genre

Mike Kelley

I would like to say a few words about the aesthetics of the period from the mid-60s to the mid-70s, in regard to images of gender confusion. This period, which, for want of a better term, I will call 'Psychedelic' is rife with such images. I will attempt to explain why I believe this is so, and to describe some of the various operative trajectories.

I think it's best to begin by explaining where I come from and why all this has some meaning for me. Having been born in 1954, I am part of the last of the 1960s generation.

I was 14 years old in 1968, old enough to feel part of the general social turmoil, and I was the last of the generation to still be eligible for the draft in the Vietnam War. I was, in essence, really too young to be a hippie, but my worldview was very much a by-product of that movement of resistance. The 1960s were a period of immense social change and unrest in America. As a

Jack Goldstein
The Jump 1978
16mm film, colour
Duration: 26 seconds

result of this, I had nothing in common with my older siblings, eight years my senior. They were post-War; I was mediated, I was part of the TV generation, I was Pop. I didn't feel part of my family, I didn't feel part of my country; I had no sense of history: the world seemed to me a media facade, a fiction, and a pack of lies. This, I believe, is what has come to be known as the postmodern condition. This is a form of alienation quite different from post-War Existentialism, because it lacks any historical footing. There is no notion of a truth that has been lost, there is simply nothing.

Nevertheless, I was enough a part of the 1960s trajectory to involve myself, at least as a spectator, in radical politics. The local version, in the city I grew up in (Detroit, Michigan) was the White Panther Party, supposedly a white spin-off of the revolutionary Black Panther Party. In reality, they were more a branch of the Yippies: a primarily white, hedonist, anarchist group. The politics of this group consisted primarily of 'acting out' – making one's life into a kind of radical street theatre. The purpose of this exercise was to make one unfit to function in normal society, and thus to prevent one from participating in and prolonging it. As the logic went, if you consumed enough drugs you simply could not work in the military-industrial complex. The White Panthers were centered in Ann Arbor, a college town, and my interest in their activities led me to related avant-garde music, theatre, film, and political events. This is what caused me to become an artist, which is quite remarkable, since I come from a working-class background and had little or no exposure to the arts as a child.

This psychedelic culture completely changed my worldview. When I first heard psychedelic music it was as if I had discovered myself. I had never much cared for music before I heard bands like the MC5, the Stooges, the Mothers of Invention, and Jimi Hendrix. The fractured nature of this music made sense to me; it mirrored the nature of the world, as I understood it, and my psyche. Of course, as every educated person knows, this was all old hat as far as modernism goes. I mean, Cubism was invented at the turn of the century, but we are talking mass culture here, not academia. What is interesting about this particular period was that the twentieth-century avant-garde was picked up and inserted into popular culture, under the guise of radical youth culture. In one swoop, Surrealism became teenybopper culture. This was possible because the artists involved in this period of crossover still considered themselves avant-gardists; this was a notion that was still conceivable at this point. Psychedelic music was 'progressive' music; it was moving forward, formally, in concert with some notion of progressive social change. This facade quickly fell apart,

even at its beginnings, which is evident in the irony of the Camp aesthetic, but it was still operable. There are several strains within this general progressive aesthetic, and almost all of them have some link to the notion of the feminine.

The popular appeal of 1960s radical youth culture in America was very much a byproduct of the anti-Vietnam War movement. Complacent white youths, for the first time, found interest in politics via the threat of conscription into military service. The model for social protest at this moment was the Black Civil Rights Movement. The pacifist tendencies of Martin Luther King worked well with an antiwar message. It was this coincidental meeting of these two very different constituencies that provoked, I believe, a full-scale empathic connection in white youth for 'otherness' in general. But the greatest Other was woman. If America's problem was that it was militaristic, patriarchal, and male, then the antidote would be the embrace of the prototypically feminine. Radical culture of this period is dominated by displays of femininity as a sign of resistance-femininity, and male homosexuality as well, for the two are conflated in the popular mind. If the female is Other, then the homosexual is doubly Other since he is 'unnatural'. I could make the claim that the Vietnam War itself promoted this posture, since one way to escape the draft was to play gay. Perhaps this is the root of the next ten years of popular homosexual posturing that finds its apex in glam rock.

Hippie and flower child culture are the 'natural' versions of this dyad of the feminine and the homosexual, and is its unnatural cousin. They share many surface similarities yet they are aesthetically opposed, despite the fact that they are both generally 'progressive' and 'leftist'. Jack Smith is a good person to talk through these issues with. Smith is the godfather of the New York 1960s avant-garde theatre and film scene. He was a major influence on a diverse set of New York trends, amazingly influencing both the Minimalist and Maximalist camps. Warhol's films and the theatre of Robert Wilson would almost be inconceivable without him. Yet what he is most famous for is making the first avant-garde transvestite film, *Flaming Creatures*, a kind of structuralist parody of Hollywood Orientalist films of the 1940s. Smith revels in the phoniness of these films. This embrace of phoniness is the essence, and politic, of the Camp aesthetic. This is an aesthetic that is, itself, suspect, for you are never sure whether its joys are real or ironic. Camp is an arcane aesthetic. Hippie culture, similarly, embraced non-Western cultures, mixing them together in a general psychedelic stew, just as Smith did. But the hippie aesthetic has a stake in truth; truth is to be found in the Other, which is our saviour. There is no room for irony in this position. Yet this essentialist position is itself suspect, for the Other in hippie culture is generally presented through cliches of the exotic. Thus, hippie aesthetics now seem kitsch, even if that was not the intention. Hippie has become Camp by default.

The pastiche aesthetic is the primary signifier of psychedelic culture. It is one that promotes confusion, while at the same time postulating equality; all parts in chaos are equal. This stance could be understood as either very democratic or, on the other hand, nihilistic. I could describe the difference as being one of a 'utopian' versus a 'black' version of Camp. The Cockettes and the films of Steven Arnold are a good place to start relative to a discussion of this difference. The Cockettes were a San Francisco-based theatre troupe who produced a kind of campy and parodistic transvestite theatre. But unlike traditional transvestite shows, they reveled in the exhibition of the incomplete pose. Though they wore extravagant costumes that mimicked Hollywood notions of glamour, this was done in a purposely poor, halfaccomplished, way. The 'queens' often had beards – a definite 'no no' in transvestite acts where 'passing' as a woman is the sign of quality. The cast members of the Cockettes included women as well as men, yet they did not often cross dress as men. The general aesthetic of the group seemed to be an attempt at a redefinition of glamour, an 'alien' glamour if you will, but one still rooted in a feminine pose. This is the group's debt to hippie culture. They represent a true crossover between hippie communalism and a later, more overtly defined, 'queer' aesthetic.

In John Waters's films, by way of comparison, there is no vestige of hippie left. Yet there is a similar play with gender slippage in the figure of the grotesque 'drag queen' Divine, who could never be mistaken for a woman. 'Queerness' is celebrated for its abject nature in American society. There is no search for an outside aesthetic, because 'you', the supposedly empathic film viewer, already represent the Other. The negative connotations of being 'artistic', that is, pathological, are presented in Waters's films in a completely unsublimated way. These are low comedies with no ascendant intentions and no redeeming social value: they are post-avant-garde and proto-punk.

The Mothers of Invention have an abject aesthetic similar in some ways to that of Waters, yet they are more traditionally avant-garde. The Mothers were a rock band formed by white R&B musician Frank Zappa in the mid-1960s. Zappa, under the influence of new music composer Edgard Varkse, combined dissonance with his R&B roots. The music of this band exemplifies the psychedelic aesthetic in its use of pastiche structures, combining elements of pop, rock, free jazz, new

Lynda Benglis
Proto Knot 1971
Wire mesh, cotton bunting, plaster, gesso and sparkles

MC5, *Kick out the Jams* 1968 (LP, Elektra)

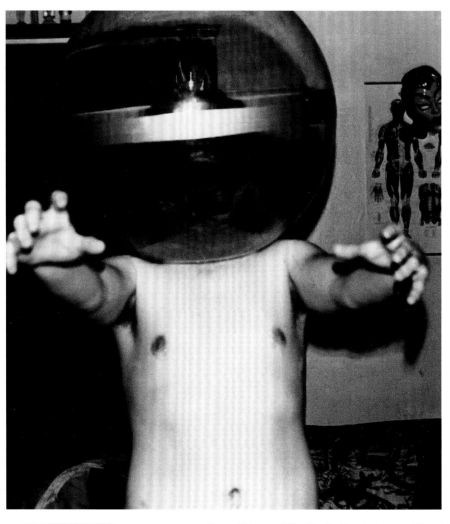

Destroy All Monsters (Mike Kelley, Jim Shaw, Cary Loren and Niagara)

Cary Loren
Jim Shaw as a Spaceman, God's Oasis 1975

Left: Cary Loren
Destroy All Monsters (Jim Shaw, Ron Asheton and Mike Kelley, at the Second Chance, Ann Arbor (performance of 'New Order') 1975

Right: Cary Loren
Niagara in Wedding Dress 1975

Below: Cary Loren
Niagara in Concoon, Wizard Robe and Sun Spots 1975

Bottom: Cary Loren
Niagara as the Great Sphinx ('Queen of Egypt' series)
1975

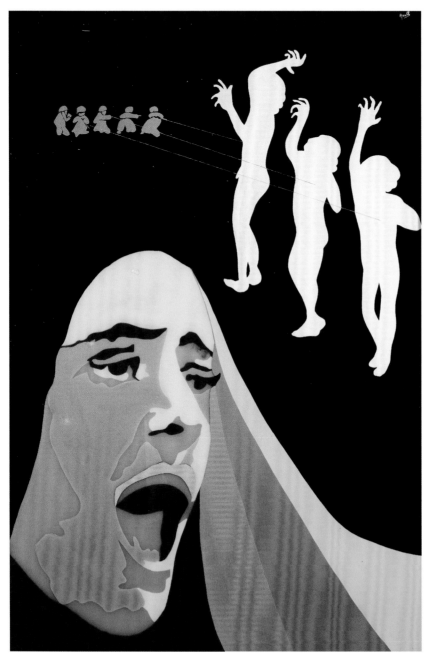

Evelyne Axell
Top: *Angela Davies II* 1972
Felt pen and crayon on cut and glued paper on metalized paper

Left: *Campus* 1970
Plexiglas and Formica

music, electronic music, and comedy. The effect is akin to a live performance of a tape collage work by John Cage. They were also overtly theatrical, adopting the transgressive stage approaches utilized in such modernist, post-Brechtian, theatrical forms as the Happening. Audience baiting and performative discontinuity are examples of their trangressive stage manner. Their visual aesthetic was neo-Dada, an abject junk aesthetic of the ugly. The Mothers were part of a larger community of musicians and artists in the Los Angeles area, centered primarily around Zappa, called the 'Freak Scene' which openly positioned itself in contrast to the hippie aesthetic of the natural. This scene included the avant-rock groups Captain Beefheart, Alice Cooper, and the GTOs – an all female band composed of groupies. All of these acts employed drag elements from time to time.

As in the Cockettes, the Mothers's version of drag was an incomplete version. But there are differences. The Cockettes, despite the ridiculous nature of their image, have a playful and positive quality that is absent in the Mothers. The Mothers's use of drag has more in common with the traditional comedic adoption of female garb by the male, and in that sense it is an abject usage. In Western culture, men who dress in female clothes are considered funny, while the opposite is generally not the case. A woman dressed in male clothes has little comedic value. The sexism at the root of this difference is obvious, for why else should the adoption of feminine characteristics by a man be abject. This is not to say that the Mothers were not a politically conscious band: the opposite is the case – they were one of the most politically conscious musical groups of the period. But they were, in a sense, a realist band that ridiculed the romantic utopianism and exoticism of hippie psychedelia. Their satiric ugliness was meant to be a distorted mirroring of the values of dominant culture.

Alice Cooper is somewhat similar, but more Pop – that is, the aesthetic is more flat; they are less open in their intentions. Their early records, like Zappa's, are a mixture of rock and roll and noise elements influenced by avant-garde music. There is a similar anti-hippie reveling in the aesthetics of the ugly – in their case this is a mix of transvestism and cheap horror film theatrics. This 'decadence', this mixture of horrific and homosexual signification, was designed for a much more general audience than Zappa's music was. Like John Waters, they were unapologetic in their embrace of the low. It could be said that they were the first truly popular Camp band, with two separate audiences. Alice Cooper was a truly successful pop band, with a string of top ten hits which included ironic saccharine ballads that some of their audience recognized as parodies, and which

others embraced as truly emotional. Similarly, some of their audience empathized with their freakish 'decadent' personas, while others perceived these roles as, simply, comedic. In this sense, because of their use of Camp strategies, Alice Cooper could be said to have outed the spectacular aspects of pop music.

Pop music in the United States has long embraced the 'glamorous', a.k.a. the homosexual, in closeted terms. Liberace's Campy stage act was never openly discussed relative to his homosexuality. He himself prevented such discussions. Liberace won a lawsuit against a British gossip columnist who only intimated that he was a homosexual. This trajectory of sublimation continues in rock and roll, which is ironic considering the 'sexual' nature of it as a musical form. Elvis was repellant at first to his primarily country music audience because of his use of make-up, but as he became more and more of a popular figure this aspect of his stage act became naturalized. The so-called British Invasion bands of the mid-1960s, like the Rolling Stones, picked up on this 'glamorous' posturing, filtering it through English visual tropes of foppish 'decadence'. Mick Jagger's stage movements were at once 'black' and 'gay' which made him doubly evil, and sexualized, in the eyes of his teenybopper fans. This posturing signals a major change in the pop arena, for the open play with 'evil' is something that Elvis, in his desire to be a mainstream pop star, would never have entertained. It was only within the framework of the 1960s counterculture that such a 'transgressive' aesthetic could find acceptance as 'pop' music.

From Jagger on, there are a string of figures who up the ante on this mix of 'decadence' and danger. The two most important are probably Jim Morrison of the Doors, and Iggy Pop of the Stooges. Morrison is said to have lifted his leather-boy look from the rough trade posturings of the Warhol scene, and his confrontational stage act from the methods of the Living Theatre. Iggy Pop's vile and self-destructive stage persona became the model for the later Punk Rock performers of the 1970s. Much of these aesthetics of 'homosexual evil', in American culture at least, can be traced back to the work of filmmaker Kenneth Anger. Anger's book *Hollywood Babylon*, which focuses on the dark and degraded sub-history of Hollywood glamour, is the bible of Camp. And his films detailing various American subcultures, seen through a homosexual gaze, set the standard for much Pop art following in the Warholian tradition. It is through Kenneth Anger that the leather-clad 1950s juvenile delinquent, and his emotion-laden songs, finds his way into the Camp pantheon, enters the Velvet Underground, and rests finally in the leather uniform of Punk. It is through him that the macho posturings of the biker thug become the sign of the alienated and sensitive artist. Consider Patti Smith's image mix of leather boy and romantic poet. Likewise, it is through Anger, whose interest in subcultural ritual led him to an interest in ritual magic, that Satanism, as another sign of decadence, enters the pop music world – primarily through the Rolling Stones in their psychedelic period when they adopt his look lock-stock-and-barrel.

What becomes of this 'outing' of the culturally agreed-upon abject nature of the feminine? As this 'transvestational' counterculture trajectory leaves the utopianism of the 1960s behind and enters the economically harsher social climate of the 1970s, two major trends emerge: feminism and Punk. With all of this feminine posturing going on, it only makes sense that women artists would finally demand to have a say in it. As I said before, even though there were women in such 'transvestite-oriented groups as the Cockettes or the various versions of the Ridiculous Theatre in New York, the outward sign of most of the costuming was gendered feminine. In discussion with some of these women artists, they describe their experience in these theatre companies as being one of self-exploration in terms of their relation to glamour. As part of the general anti-patriarchal thrust of the period these women were not particularly interested in playing with the adoption of male gender stereotypes. Mary Woronov is the exception here, with her overtly S&M persona as the whip dancer with the Velvet Underground, her 'butch' roles in Warhol's films, and her masculine portrayals in John Vaccaro's productions.

But more often, these women were more concerned with their own relationship to feminine stereotypes. The GTOs, for example, invented a look that was a trash version of the female Hollywood stars of the 1920s and 1930s. Like the Warhol 'Star System', this was meant to be a retooling, a redefinition of that beauty, yet still tied to it through the inversions of Camp. Various women artists in the early 1970s began to play with shifting roles and identities in relation to issues of glamour and gender. Eleanor Antin did a work, *Representational Painting*, where she sat in front of a mirror applying makeup, removing it, and applying it again in a constant state of 'pictorial' self-definition. She later adopted a series of overtly theatrical personas, including a king, a nurse, and a ballerina. This kind of play reached its zenith in Judy Chicago's feminist workshop programs in the Los Angeles area in the early 1970s. Here, women artists collectively explored their relationship to various feminine stereotypes in a much more critical and politically conscious environment than had previously been done. Performances were made utilizing such stereotypes as the cheerleader, bride, waitress, beauty queen, and drag queen, as a way of exploring and doing battle with them.

Concurrent with this movement was the rise of glam rock. I would say, at least in America, that Alice Cooper is the transitional figure here. He is the figure who leaves psychedelia behind and fully embraces the Pop framework – trying to balance irony and popular appeal. Glam rock was a music that fully understood the commercial music world and accepted it as an arena of facade and emptiness. It used the image of the drag queen as a sign of this status. David Bowie is the great example here. He adopts and throws away personas as the seasons change, always reinventing himself for the market. In this sense, he is a mirror of our culture of planned obsolescence. The argument has been put forth that, in relation to consumer culture, the constantly changing chameleon persona is empowerment. Madonna's practice has been discussed this way in certain feminist contexts, though I personally have grave misgivings about this reading of her practice, just as I do of Bowie's. She becomes the sign of a spectacular female producer in contrast to the traditional image of the passive female consumer. I might add that this is how the GTOs thought of themselves: as consumers, groupies who became producers, rock stars themselves. The spectacular is tackled head on.

Punk was the immediate answer to this fixation with spectacular consumer culture; it replaced the spectacular with the pathetic. Punk was the last gasp of avant gardeism in Pop, played out with the most extreme signs of decadent nihilism. As a symbol of this 'end state', the gender signification of the previous avant-garde was reversed: maleness became the general referent. The Punk uniform is the macho rough trade look of Kenneth Anger's Camp leather boy, for men and women alike. Androgyny remains a factor here. Whether this 'unisex' approach was a vestige of some connection to the utopianism of the feminine androgyny of the psychedelic period, or is simply consistent with the capitalist cult of youth culture, is open to argument. But that is another story.

This paper was originally presented on 26 September 1999 in Graz, Austria at the Steirischer Herbst festival as part of 'Re-Make/Re-Model: Secret Histories of Art, Pop, Life and the Avantgarde', a series of panel discussions sponsored by the Berlin Group and the Steirischer Herbst.

Ed Paschke
Machino 1976
Oil on canvas

The Rift of Retro: 1962? Or Twenty Years On?

Simon Reynolds

In his 1970 book *Revolt Into Style*, George Melly describes pop culture as 'the country of "Now"' and argues that the nation of youth 'denies having any history. The words "Do you remember" are the filthiest in its language.' But how then to explain the 'eclectic nostalgia' of psychedelia, the Edwardiana and Victoriana that pervaded record covers and posters and pop groups' clothing? Melly insists that this isn't nostalgia at all but rather 'a subtle method of rejecting the past', all that unavoidably omnipresent history surrounding British kids as they grow up. 'Wrenching these objects out of their historical context' turns them from totems into relics. Sifting through the antique shops and Portobello-style street markets for bric-a-brac, bohemian hipsters reduced history to 'a vast boutique full of military uniforms, grannie shoes and spectacles, 1930s suits and George Formby records.'[1] The past became a plaything for a present-minded generation.

Mick Rock
David Bowie, Earl's Court 1973
Archival digital print

What's different about glam, and what constituted a break with the 1960s, is that it was rock's *own* past that got revisited and recycled. Instead of the blithe impertinence of psychedelia, there was a spectrum of attitudes ranging from reverence and yearning nostalgia to camp and irony. Although Pop art was an influence (mostly indirectly, but also directly in the case of Roxy Music, through Richard Hamilton's tutelage of Bryan Ferry), this self-reflexive and *retro*spective tendency seems to have generated itself spontaneously. Glam points to a peculiar susceptibility within pop to becoming enthralled by its own archive of stylised images and period-specific sounds, a latent capacity to fold back on its own history.

Glam was not the first rock movement, though, to reach what I call 'the Rift of Retro'. It was closely entwined with an earlier backward-looking tendency in pop history, the 1950s rock and roll revival, which is usually associated with the early 1970s but which actually began in 1968. After the excesses of psychedelia, there was a feeling in the air of 'rock and roll's coming back'. By 1969, it was definitely 'in': Jeff Beck hastily added covers of Elvis Presley's 'All Shook Up' and 'Jailhouse Rock' to his second album *Beck-ola*; the cover of the Aynsley Dunbar Retaliation's album *To Mum, from Aynsley and the Boys* featured Dunbar and his band dressed as Teddy Boys, with Brylcreemed quiffs and drape jackets, and Jimi Hendrix produced the Cat Mother single 'Good Old Rock and Roll'.

Another beneficiary of Hendrix's patronage was Sha Na Na, a rock revival troupe formed by students at Columbia University. Blown away by their campy recreation of 1950s stage routines, the acid-rock god wangled them onto the bill at Woodstock. A merging of Pop art and parody, Sha Na Na was the brainchild of cultural history student George Leonard, a Warhol admirer who was also acquainted with Susan Sontag's essay 'Notes on "Camp"' (1964). Leonard has described the group's rendition of the 1959 hit 'Teen Angel' as 'a danced Lichtenstein, pose by pose', suggesting that Sha Na Na's version bears the same relation to the original that Lichtenstein's paintings bore to the comic strip panels. But where Pop art translated the logos and images of commerce and mass entertainment into high-cultural artefacts, the move made by Sha Na Na – and, within a few years, by glam's retro-pasticheurs – stayed within the domain of pop.

Strangely, the rock and roll revival's reversal of the forward march of the 1960s was launched by two of the artists most associated with innovation, the Beatles and Frank Zappa. These arch-progressives pioneered regressive rock: the Beatles with 'Back in the USSR', a pastiche of Chuck Berry and early Beach Boys, and Zappa with his doo-wop project 'Cruising with

Reuben and the Jets', which adapted the imaginary group concept of *Sgt. Pepper's Lonely Hearts Club Band* to overtly nostalgic ends.

'Back in the USSR' opened *The Beatles*, a.k.a. the White Album (1968). When writing about the album in his 1969 book *The Story of Rock*, Carl Belz gets close to formulating the concept of postmodernism. Defending the record's self-conscious references to the Beach Boys, Chuck Berry, Bob Dylan, and even earlier stages of the Beatles' own music, Belz notes that the Fab Four 'are going back over musical territory which they have already covered, which they already know, and which they have left.'[2] By abandoning the modernist (and progressive rock) credo that earlier styles of rock become definitively superseded (cf. Hendrix's 'you'll never hear surf music again') and that the true artist keeps moving on and never reverts to an earlier stage of his or her own development, the Beatles questioned 'the idea of progress' in rock.

Some of the rare negative verdicts on the White Album also anticipate the idea of postmodernism. *New Left Review*'s Richard Merton disparaged the record as a sterile spectacle of 'musical radicalism, robbed of its object, revolving on itself. The outcome is logically self-subversion: parody and pastiche', with innovation and originality supplanted by 'a circular process of more or less competent mimicry.'[3] Bizarrely, 'Richard Merton' was the rock-critic pseudonym of Perry Anderson, the Marxist theorist who later wrote a superior dissection of postmodernity, *The Origins of Postmodernism* (1998). Did he ever subsequently realise just how near his youthful alter ego got to identifying the postmodern condition, and critiquing it, before it even really existed?

It could be that the Rift of Retro is inherent and latent in any cultural formation. Jazz's own fold-back occurred in the 1980s with Wynton Marsalis's neoclassicism. That term echoes the neoclassical school of the 1920s and 1930s, when composers such as Stravinsky and Milhaud embraced the formal constraints of eighteenth-century idioms. It seems that any field of artistic endeavour reaches a point at which it has accumulated so much history behind it that the archives exert a gravitational pull, which becomes increasingly irresistible as the various pathways into the future become dead ends of ugliness and difficulty. At this point an emerging artist can 'go forward' in terms of his or her individual trajectory only by going back. 'Originality' becomes a strategy of self-differentiation against one's contemporaries through artful choices within the repertoire of non-contemporary styles. Creativity becomes curatorial and recombinant; mastery

Mick Rock
Dude 1972
Archival digital print

equates with detail-oriented, perfectionist craft rather than messy expressive vision.

At the time Belz and Merton/Anderson were writing – around the same time that Bowie, Ferry and other key glam figures such as Alice Cooper and Marc Bolan were formulating their ideas – the term 'postmodernist' barely existed. It was just beginning to be hatched within a rarefied milieu of architectural critics and art theorists. Pop music found its own way there, assisted by its innate capacities for nostalgia and for self-mockery, its twin flairs for sentimental reverence and sacrilegious irreverence.

Surveying glam's 1971–75 heyday reveals a spectrum of retro and revivalist modes.

PRIMALISM

On the silver-foil surface, Gary Glitter appears to be the Sha Na Na principle amplified to a grotesque degree: an overblown farrago of kitsch costumes, butch postures, mincing mock-menace. Glitter's career began and ended in revivalism. He first performed under the Glitter alias at the London Rock and Roll Show, a huge revivalist festival at Wembley Stadium in August 1972, where he played on the same bill as legends such as Little Richard (and drew inspiration for his image from the mirrored jacket that Richard wore that day). In his twilight as pop idol, Glitter's chart hits slip into the same sorry zone of 1950s rehash as those of Showaddywaddy. But if you ignore the visuals and *listen* to Glitter's early hits, such as 'Hello, Hello, I'm Back Again' and 'I'm the Leader of the Gang (I Am)', you hear lyrics that obsessively reference rock and roll (his first two hits were 'Rock and Roll' and 'I Didn't Know I Loved You ('Til I Saw You Rock and Roll)') but music that doesn't replicate or reiterate that of the 1950s. Instead Glitter and producer Mike Leander attempted to achieve the same level of impact – in terms of primal incitement – that rock and roll had in 1956, but through radically updated means. Influenced by Afro-rock, Dr. John and James Brown, it's an intimidatingly minimal sound that evokes the Brutalist tower blocks and concrete youth centres of 1970s Britain, not the jukebox halls and 1950s Americana alluded to in the lyrics.

The Gary Glitter releases were studio creations, built around an astonishingly punishing and dead-eyed drum sound, ominous swoops of treated guitar, gang chants, and empty space. 'We wanted to make it purely a tune and rhythm with no embellishments like harmonies or chords' said Leander, describing 'Rock and Roll, Part 1' and 'Part 2', the two sides of Glitter's breakthrough single.[4] A journalist for *Let It Rock* put it more bluntly, describing 'Part 2' – the near-instrumental B-side

that took off in the discotheques – as 'a castration op where you throw away the patient and keep the balls.'[5] Glitter himself spoke of his singing and performance in terms of a barbarian minimalism, stating 'my music is purely physical. It's vulgar. It's crude. It's raw.'[6] Separated from the preposterous splendour of the costumes, the Naked Ape embarrassment of chest hair, Glitterbeat doesn't sound retro: it suggests rather the rebirth of rock and roll's savage spirit in a new decade and a different country, the harsh urban landscape of 1970s Britain.

CONSCIOUS CAMP

Camp, as defined by Susan Sontag, is an aesthetic of consumption, not of production: it's a sensibility that is attracted to pop culture performers (in music, movies, etc.) who are excessively stylised, but who enter into the artifice with total commitment, a passion that seems to be untouched by the very knowingness and detachment that marks the connoisseur of camp. Camp is a schizoid pleasure, a mixed emotion: the appreciator of camp is simultaneously amused by the absurdity and moved by the sincerity. There is a revelling in the historicity, the datedness of the form, even as the performer inhabits it not as *a* style but as Style: the 'natural' and timelessly right way of expressing that emotion.

Camp is complex enough as a consumer sensibility, but attempting to create camp – to make work that will have the camp effect on viewers and listeners – is even more infolded with irony. It stages a split within utterance itself, a 'scare-quotes'-like hedging or standing-outside. We have become used to this kind of thing from mainstream pop in the last few decades (Robbie Williams rolling his eyes while singing as if to undercut the otherwise earnest rendition, or seeking to entertain us with a song called 'Let Me Entertain You'). But when Roxy Music did it in the early 1970s, it was new and startling; to some, unnerving, even a sign of decadence.

Conscious camp is not always tied to retro: Roxy songs such as 'Beauty Queen' and 'If There Is Something' achieve the effect through the jolting disparity between the evident passion and Ferry's delivery and lyrics: disproportionately florid and imagistic with 'Beauty Queen', sliding into Valentine's card triteness mingled with bathos on 'If There Is Something', where Ferry's amorous pledges of devotion climax with the promise to 'grow potatoes by the score'. But sometimes conscious camp entails retro moves. The second half of 'In Every Dream Home a Heartache' is both genuinely psychedelic and 'psychedelic', deploying circa-1967 clichés such as phasing on the drums and guitar, the trick fade/surprise return of the song, and so forth. Another example, drawn from Roxy's visual presentation, is the front sleeve of their eponymous debut album, the first in a series of cover photographs of lingerie-clad models: the shot of Kari-Ann Muller styled as a 1940s pin-up is designed to be both titillating and *très amusant*, the two modes of enjoyment undercutting each other in same way that vintage porn incites the viewer to have a 'wistful wank'.

Conscious camp often verges on outright comedy. Roxy guitarist Phil Manzanera has talked of how there was 'a lot of humour [...] a lot of piss-taking' of styles such as heavy rock in the band's music.[7] Brian Eno, their synth player, admired rock parodists the Bonzo Dog Doo-Dah Band and participated in the Portsmouth Sinfonia, an orchestra in which everybody played an instrument in which they weren't fully proficient, resulting in hilariously wonky versions of well-known classical pieces. Parody, in a sense, offers a 'legitimate' form of what would otherwise be merely redundant, uninspired, an act of plagiarism. Take *The Rutles*, the Beatles-inspired mockumentary with songs composed by ex-Bonzo Neil Innes. It's not so much that the satiric intent inoculates against the nostalgia, more that we enjoy *The Rutles* on several levels simultaneously: a trip down memory lane, a witty piss-take, a skilful reproduction.

Parody remained an undercurrent in Roxy Music but blossomed fully in the fellow-traveller outfit the Moodies and in *Rock Follies*, a TV satire of the music business that was almost a Roxy spin-off given that the songs were written by the group's Andy Mackay. Friends with Eno, the Moodies were a mostly female ensemble of art school graduates. Blending aspects of cabaret, pantomime, Dada, and performance art, their concerts consisted of no original songs, just cover versions of pop classics such as Presley's 'Return To Sender' or the Shangri-Las' 'Remember (Walking in the Sand)'. The Moodies' approach – 'simultaneously glorifying and ridiculing glamour', enthused *Spare Rib* – anticipated everything from Wigstock, vogueing and the drag king movement, to Cindy Sherman and the re-enactment art craze of the 2000s.[8]

Genre-blending comedy, musicals and gritty drama, *Rock Follies* followed the tortuous route to fame of Little Ladies, a band fronted by three women, across two series aired in 1976 and 1977. A mordant satire of the mid-1970s music industry, among *Follies*' targets are revivalism and nostalgia. The Little Ladies form themselves out of the cast of a doomed attempt to revive a Depression-era musical to ride 'the nostalgia wave'. One of the group, Q, is a time-warp figure herself, who wishes she lived in the era of George Gershwin and doubts she'll really fit in a rock band: 'I like rock not when it's deep but fun... camp... I

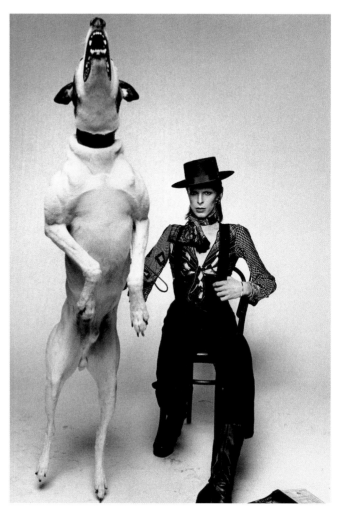

Terry O'Neill
David Bowie 1974
Bromide fibre print

Mick Rock
Ziggy Stardust Fans 1973
Archival digital print

Right:
Publicity for 'The Rock'n'Roll Show', Wembley Stadium 1972

Opposite: Mick Rock
Rock Dreams 1973
Archival digital print

Derek Boshier
Reel 1973
16mm film, colour, sound
Duration: 6 minutes

Mick Rock
David Bowie and Mick Ronson having lunch on the train to Aberdeen 1973

Iggy Pop (Four Lights) 1972
Archival digital prints

like Sha Na Na.' After various misadventures the Little Ladies fall into the clutches of aspiring record-biz mogul Stavros, who completely remakes their image. They perform the song 'Biba Nova' – a nod to the glam-era retro-fashion boutique Biba – at the nostalgia restaurant Idols. But already 'the heyday of the elegance, Bryan Ferry and his white dinner jacket' has passed, and Stavros decides that with the economy in crisis, 'Austerity Rock' will be the next big thing. The Little Ladies are remodelled as 1940s nostalgia act the Victory Girls, singing songs such as 'Where's My Gasmask', 'I'll Be a War Bride' and 'Glenn Miller is Missing'. Stavros builds Blitz Club, which is styled as a London tube station turned bomb shelter, with deliberately grotty grub purchased using a ration card, and a simulated air raid.

As it happens, Roxy's 1972 eponymous debut album featured 'The Bob (Medley)', a song-suite/soundscape/mini-movie recreation of the Battle of Britain, complete with sounds of artillery and exploding bombs. But there are also passages in 'The Bob' that sound like Black Sabbath, an oboe-laced pastoral interlude, and a West Coast hippie singalong. The track is an extreme example of a general principle that runs through Roxy's work: the musical past as a smorgasbord. 'Lennon describes his music as seventies rock,' Andy Mackay told a journalist from *Disc* in 1972. 'Ours is fifties, seventies, and eighties.' (He could equally have added 1920s, 1930s, 1940s, and 1960s.) 'It's inevitable that we're going to be influenced by lots of things, people, and ideas. The combinations are endless.'[9]

The idea is inscribed into the final stretch of 'Remake/Remodel', the mission statement opening track on Roxy Music. The other instruments cut away repeatedly to allow each player a moment in the spotlight, all of which take the form of playing highly recognisable quotes, such as the riff from the Beatles' 'Day Tripper'. 'A précis history of rock'n'roll' is how the album's producer Pete Sinfield described it, but it's more than that: Mackay's riff is the driving refrain from Wagner's *Ride of the Valkyries* rendered as King Curtis-style sax honk (a sort of double-cover: someone else's song done in another artist's style).[10]

'Do The Strand', the opener on the second album *For Your Pleasure*, spells out the idea: 'All styles served here.' There's a rejection of the idea of rejection itself: the notion that aesthetic choices are antithetical, that they represent stances and world-views that you have to buy into and adhere to. Being into rock doesn't require jettisoning the earlier pop culture of Hollywood and Broadway, or the European culture of the early twentieth century (Nijinsky, La Goulue and *Guernica* all get namechecks in the song).

The idea of non-commitment and the protean artist, pioneered by Ferry and Bowie with their image changes and serial personae, has gone on to be enormously influential. One example, from the 1980s: the career of Adam Ant, whose songs and videos ran through a series of historical costume personae that included Apache braves, pirates, highwaymen, and knights in shining armour.

Glam turns history into a wardrobe full of costumes, and as such parallels and intertwines with fashion, the first area of popular culture to succumb to retro's auto-cannibalistic archive-raiding logic. (Roxy were known for their close involvement with the designer Antony Price, who – in an unusual gesture for a rock band at that time – received credits on the album sleeves for the group's clothes, hair and make-up.) Remembering her time in the Moodies, Anne Bean – now a performance and installation artist – spoke of being 'very interested in what style was [...] you saw these people like Rothko and Beuys who had this very definite style. [But] I couldn't imagine what my style would be, because I *loved everything* [...] I liked that idea of being lots of different people.'[11] Self-reinvention offered both freedom and relief from the pressure to commit. But Quentin Crisp had a different perspective, decreeing that true style is 'deciding who you are and being able to perpetuate it', whereas 'fashion is never having to decide who you are.'[12]

Glam's various retro modes, and its overlap with the larger rock and roll revival, suggest that rock is neither modernist nor postmodernist but both simultaneously. The very now-ness of pop in the 1960s that George Melly identified contains within itself a date-stamp, which inevitably goes on to engender nostalgia, in much the same way that an individual in middle age looking back wistfully to adolescence or childhood is partly being nostalgic for a time when he or she wasn't nostalgic, but lived fully in the present.

Former members of Roxy Music separately touched on this paradox in 1976–77, at a time when punk resurrected the teenage now-consciousness of the 1960s (the Clash's 'No Elvis, Beatles or the Rolling Stones in 1977') but in appropriately apocalyptic form (the Sex Pistols' 'No Future'). In the supergroup 801, Phil Manzanera and Brian Eno covered the Beatles' radically futuristic 1966 track 'Tomorrow Never Knows' (whose title derived from a saying of Ringo Starr's, equivalent to the 1960s maxim 'be here now'). Bryan Ferry's solo single 'This Is Tomorrow' took its title from the 1956 Whitechapel Art Gallery exhibition, the public launch of the British branch of Pop art, which offered a preview of the 1960s. Flashbacks to flashforwards, these forgotten songs capture the contradiction of retro, which is dependent on the *un*-retro: moments of nowness and newness that then get forever trapped in the amber of the archives. The very technologies of recording that enabled pop to achieve global ubiquity also allowed its peaks to be repeated long after the event, to become fixated on by fans.

1 George Melly, *Revolt Into Style: The Pop Arts*, London: Allen Lane – The Penguin Press, 1970, pp. 6–7.
2 Carl Belz, 'Rock and Fine Art', extract from *The Story of Rock*, Oxford: Oxford University Press, 1969, reprinted in Mike Evans, ed., *The Beatles Literary Anthology*, London: Plexus, 2004, pp. 289–95.
3 Richard Merton, 'Comment on Chester's "For a Rock Aesthetic"', *The New Left Review* I/59, January–February 1970, pp. 88–96.
4 Mike Leander, in Paul Oldfield, 'Glitter', *Monitor*, no. 4, October 1985.
5 Unattributed, in ibid.
6 Gary Glitter, in ibid.
7 Phil Manzanera, in Paul Auslander, *Performing Glam Rock*, Ann Arbor: University of Michigan Press, p. 159.
8 *Spare Rib* reviewer, unattributed, in Moodies feature by Adrian Whittaker with Michael Bracewell, 'Non-stop Exotic Cabaret', *The Wire* no. 313, March 2010, pp. 39–40.
9 Andy Mackay, in David Buckley, *The Thrill of It All: Bryan Ferry & Roxy Music*, Chicago: Chicago Review Press, 2005, p. 72.
10 Pete Sinfield, in Buckley, *The Thrill of It All*, p. 68.
11 Anne Bean, in Whittaker with Bracewell, 'Non-stop Exotic Cabaret', p. 43.
12 Quentin Crisp, in Paul Morley, *Ask: The Chatter of Pop*, London: Faber & Faber, 1986, p. 16.

ocking while Rome Burns: The Politics of Glam

Alwyn W. Turner

Despite its early promise, 1968 was a year of defeats and setbacks for the political left. The Prague Spring was crushed by Soviet tanks, the French general strike was followed by a massive victory for the Gaullist party in parliamentary elections, and in America Richard Nixon was elected president, while Martin Luther King and Bobby Kennedy were both murdered. In Britain the rightwing reaction was less dramatic, though the massive popular support for Enoch Powell's 'rivers of blood' speech offered clear evidence of a potential backlash against the forces of progress that had dominated the 1960s thus far. An opinion poll showed 75 per cent of the country agreeing with Powell's views on immigration, and two years later he helped Edward Heath's Conservatives to a surprise general election victory.[1]

Pop music, so often the bellwether of British social trends, had already registered the change in mood. Despite

Nancy Hellebrand
Lesley Kelley, an audio typist, Somers Town 1973
Silver gelatin print on paper

being remembered as the year of psychedelia, 1967 had been dominated by a surge in easy-listening. The Beatles' *Sergeant Pepper* album was outsold in Britain by the soundtracks to *The Sound of Music* and *Dr. Zhivago* and by a Herb Alpert album released in January of the previous year. In the week that Scott McKenzie's 'San Francisco (Be Sure to Wear Flowers in your Hair)' went to no. 1, the government pulled the plugs on the pirate radio stations. The decade-long march of progressive liberalism was halted, along with the ever more experimental rock and roll that had provided its soundtrack. There was a feeling that, politically and culturally, the vanguard had become stranded from its followers. Puzzled by the apparent failure of the debut album by Country Joe & the Fish, the disc jockey John Peel asked the group's record company: 'Why isn't this in the charts? Everybody I know has a copy.' The truth, he subsequently realised, 'was the other way round: I knew everybody who'd got a copy.'[2]

The response of the leading rock acts was to return to basics, to the rock and roll of the Beatles' 'Lady Madonna' and the Rolling Stones' 'Jumpin' Jack Flash', and to the country-folk of Bob Dylan's *John Wesley Harding*. The de-politicis-ation of rock was inherited by the new wave of British artists who broke through in the early 1970s. 'No one thinks of pop music as a call to arms any more,' wrote George Melly in 1973. 'The musicians have joined the acceptance world.'[3] He was quite correct, at least in relation to glam, where politics were consciously avoided in favour of a studied celebration of rock and roll that was both ironic and enthusiastic. Roxy Music offered 'a danceable solution to teenage revolution,'[4] echoing the message of David Bowie's messianic 'Starman' ('Let the children boogie'[5]), while Marc Bolan's message was simpler still: 'You can bump and grind, it is good for your mind.'[6] Bowie in particular was to return repeatedly to political non-involvement in this era, whether dismissing 'that revolution stuff'[7] or reflecting on post-war socialism: 'Bevan tried to change the nation,' he shrugged, 'but I could make a transformation as a rock and roll star.'[8]

And yet, unlike the 1960s, these were times when troubles were undoubtedly rising. In 1972, the year that glam took over the British charts, the number of working days lost to strikes reached nearly 24 million, ten times the level of 1966, and more than in any year since the 1926 general strike. It was a year that saw unemployment reach a million for the first time since the wartime army had been demobbed, the government twice declare a state of emergency, and nearly five hundred people lose their lives as a result of the civil war in Northern Ireland.

Inflation was also taking a sharp upward turn; averaging four per cent a year in the second half of the 1960s, it had shot up to over ten per cent in the first half of the 1970s.

The harsh economic climate hit young people particularly hard. With record numbers of school-leavers in 1971, nine out of ten of them possessing no exam qualifications at all, the future looked bleak, so much so that the then education secretary, Margaret Thatcher, responded by raising the school leaving age to sixteen, an early attempt to manipulate unemployment figures. In this context, the overtly apolitical nature of glam might have seemed an anomaly. In fact, it suited the times perfectly.

If there was one image that dominated political discourse in the early 1970s, it was that of Weimar Germany, and the destruction wrought by uncontrolled inflation. As early as March 1970, the Labour cabinet minister Richard Crossman was claiming that the level of student demonstrations 'was like the early days of the Weimar Republic' and warning that he 'could see democracy coming to an end.'[9] Within a couple of years, the comparison had become widespread amongst commentators and politicians of all parties, from the Conservative Lord Hailsham[10] through John Pardoe of the Liberals[11] to Harold Wilson himself,[12] to the extent that the *Guardian* felt obliged to dismiss the idea: 'Talk in this country of another Weimar always seemed grotesquely exaggerated', it said in a leader column, though the fact that the theme was mentioned yet again was hardly the best way to calm fears.[13]

Nor were the associations dispelled by the huge success of the musical *Cabaret*, based on Christopher Isherwood's 1939 novel *Goodbye to Berlin*. The first London staging was in 1968, a production starring Judi Dench, but the greatest impact was made by the 1972 film with Liza Minnelli, which opened in Britain in the same month that Tony Richardson's production of Bertolt Brecht and Kurt Weill's *The Threepenny Opera* hit the West End stage, with a cast that included Vanessa Redgrave and Barbara Windsor. The popular conception of the fourteen-year-long Weimar Republic centred on the combination of hyperinflation and decadent theatricality, of a nation adopting the alleged pose of Nero during the Great Fire of Rome. The Britain of the early 1970s looked back at the era and, with a certain sense of self-dramatisation, saw its own future reflected.

Into this world came glam and it didn't for a moment look out of place. There were explicit musical references, from the Sensational Alex Harvey Band's cover of *Cabaret*'s 'Tomorrow Belongs to Me' to Roxy Music's Brecht/Weill tribute 'Bitter-Sweet' ('das ist nicht das Ende der Welt' barked Ferry,

Above: Nancy Hellebrand
Dave Fowle Sr and Dave Fowle Jnr 1973
Silver gelatin print on paper

Top right: Nancy Hellebrand
Dave and a friend 1973
Silver gelatin print on paper

Right: Nancy Hellebrand
Delia (Marc Bolan fan in her Bedroom) 1973
Silver gelatin print on paper

Peter Phillips
Six Times Eight, Dreaming 1974
Lithograph on paper

over a goose-stepping rhythm that made it sound as though it probably was.)[14] Then there were the lyrical name-droppings that culminated in the bleakness of Lou Reed's 1973 album *Berlin*. And above all there was the figure of Ziggy Stardust himself, the sexually ambivalent creature singing of darkness, disgrace and dismay to *femmes fatales*, the spirit of Berlin cabaret writ large in a pre-apocalyptic world with just 'five years left to cry in.'[15] The subtitle of Bowie's song 'Aladdin Sane (1913–1938–197?)' spelt out the feeling that society was on the brink of complete collapse.

In his novel *Steppenwolf*, published at the height of Weimar and rediscovered by the 1960s counterculture, Hermann Hesse wrote of the 'shrill and blood-raw music' that was popular at the time: 'One half of this music, the melody, was all pomade and sugar and sentimentality. The other half was savage, temperamental and vigorous.' It was as accurate a description of glam as anything that contemporary criticism offered, and glam would have enjoyed too Hesse's conclusion: 'It was the music of decline. There must have been such music in Rome under the later emperors.'[16]

As Britain descended, in the space of little more than a decade, from imperial power to its new role as 'the sick man of Europe', glam offered an escapist fantasy, mirroring a widespread loss of faith in the nation's ability to recover. The retreat from political engagement, particularly from faith in a socialist future, was expressed most clearly when Mott the Hoople included on the sleeve of their album *Mott* the text of D.H. Lawrence's poem 'A Sane Revolution'. Written in the aftermath of the General Strike, the poem argued that, if there were to be a revolution, it should be a purely personal expression of freedom:

> *Don't do it for the working classes.*
> *Do it so that we can all of us be little*
> *aristocracies on our own*
> *and kick our heels like jolly escaped asses.*

In essence that was the promise of glam, the realisation of Aleister Crowley's dictum: 'Every man and every woman a star.'[17] If society couldn't be transformed in the public sphere, it could at least be transcended in private.

Mott was released in July 1973, the month that the British economy officially went into recession. From here on, times got truly difficult. By the end of the year, an oil crisis and a miners' overtime ban had plunged Britain into yet another state of emergency. Industry was put on a three-day week, street lighting and the motorway speed limit were reduced, and television broadcasts were closed down at 10.30 pm, all in an

effort to save fuel. The government's slogan ('SOS – Switch Off Something Now') only heightened the sense of a country that had finally arrived at the long-promised crisis.

In this new world, the deliberate detachment of glam was difficult to maintain. 'The country has never been in such a state since the war' said Brian Connolly of the Sweet,[18] and others queued up to share similar thoughts with the music papers. 'We've gone back to the Middle Ages in a week!' marvelled Ian Hunter of Mott the Hoople. 'One minute it's 1973 – now it's 1073.'[19] Time was running out for glam. One of the many strikes of 1974 came that summer when television technicians blacked out all live programmes for several weeks, including *Top of the Pops*. A style that relied heavily on its televisual appeal, glam could not long survive without the oxygen of publicity. The more artistically inclined acts – most notably David Bowie and Roxy Music – were already looking towards soul and dance music as the way forward, a chance to distance themselves from the less cerebral bands that had become associated with the glam genre. For those who remained, there was a certain irony that a pop phenomenon that had so deliberately turned its back on politics was ultimately to be brought down by industrial action.

1 Cited in Arthur Marwick, *The Pelican Social History of Britain: British Society Since 1945*, London: Penguin, 1982, p. 169.
2 Jonathan Green, *Days in the Life: Voices from the English Underground 1961–1971*, London: Pimlico, 1998, p. 187.
3 *Observer* colour supplement, 7 October 1973.
4 Bryan Ferry, 'Do the Strand', E.G. Music Ltd, 1973.
5 David Bowie, 'Starman', Mainman/Chrysalis Music Ltd, 1972.
6 Marc Bolan, 'Children of the Revolution', Wizard Publishing Ltd, 1972.
7 David Bowie, 'All the Young Dudes', Mainman/Chrysalis Music Ltd, 1972.
8 David Bowie, 'Star', Mainman/Chrysalis Music Ltd, 1972.
9 Tony Benn, *Office without Power*, London: Arrow, 1989.
10 *The Times*, 19 November 1970.
11 *The Guardian*, 27 June 1972.
12 *The Observer*, 9 September 1973.
13 *The Guardian*, 3 March 1971.
14 Bryan Ferry/Andy Mackay, 'Bitter-Sweet', E.G. Music Ltd, 1974.
15 David Bowie, 'Five Years', Mainman/Chrysalis Music Ltd, 1972.
16 Hermann Hesse, *Steppenwolf*, translated by Basil Creighton, Harmondsworth: Penguin, 1965, p. 47.
17 Aleister Crowley, *The Book of the Law*, I:3, online at www.thebookofthelaw.com/2010/11/01/liber-al-vel-legis-chapter-1.
18 *Melody Maker*, 26 January 1974.
19 *Melody Maker*, 5 January 1974.

Dennis Hutchinson
Exotic Adrian Street and his coalminer father 1973
Photograph on paper

Opposite: Bruce Lacey
Stella Superstar and Her Amazing Galactic Adventures 1973
DVD, colour, sound

Bang the Whole Gang

Neil Mulholland

Talent is relative.[1]

Despite glam rock's near ubiquity in the early 1970s, relatively few visual artists in Britain appear to have flirted with its flash trash. From the present-day perspective, much of the new art of the period was earnestly opposed to the entertainment industry. While glam rockers indulged in the overdetermined, the camp, the theatrical and the performative, contemporary artists were busy finding new ways of deconstructing mediation. Public art, cybernetic art, photoconceptualism, squat-based collectives, feminist arts organisations – all seem as far removed from glam as we can imagine. This registers visually as well as ideologically: the exhibition 'New Art' staged at the Hayward Gallery in London comprised of works that were almost all was minimal, monochromatic, linguistically turned and prosaic.[2]

Certainly, forty years ago, a dominant concern of the New Art was with subverting, demystifying and unpicking

Tim Street-Porter
Duggie Fields at Home c.1970s

the seams of a visual regime that 'naturalised' and obscured the politics of mediation.[3] As a mood of deepening socio-economic crisis swept through the first half of the decade, a social turn ensued in which semiotic analysis was applied to politicised subjects otherwise ignored or demonised by the reactionary British press. Artists began to engage directly with major sites of ideological struggle: the collapse of an optimistic oil-based economy in the wake of the Suez crisis, the oppression of women, homophobia, the Troubles in Northern Ireland, hyperinflation, the return of mass unemployment,[4] industrial action and the post-Fordist casualisation of labour.[5] This radicalised postmodernism in the art of the early 1970s provided a historical progenitor for the social turn in art during the 'long nineties'.[6] Such is the hold of the art of the 1990s, we can only imagine the art of the 1970s through the prism of a feedback loop that continues to be generated by contemporary art.[7]

While, on the face of it, glam would seem to emerge from a very different decade to the one we think we know, it shares, in theory at least, common egalitarian countercultural roots with the social turn. Like the New Art, glam was not *authentic*. In its mannerist concern with illusionism and metafiction, it was the nemesis of any pretentions to artistic authenticity. Like the New Art, glam stood against idealism and in favour of levelling the playing field of 'signifying practices', approaching culture as if it were a hermetically sealed, self-sustaining system of surfaces and signs. Talent is relative.

Glam's engagement with media diverges from the social turn only at the point of production. Where the New Art pursued a stripped-down analysis of mediation, glam focussed on its excessive overproduction. This is to say that glam's multiple and highly diversified media were part of its decadent over-identification with mediation itself. In this, glam generated an intermedial site in which art, fashion, performance, design and music could be pursued synchronously as a flamboyant performance of pop's *gesamtkunstwerk*. Surfaces and signs from the recent and distant past were *styles* to be freely sampled and remixed. Glam was a peculiar peacock restaging of the baroque ornamentation of show-business mixed with the downbeat nihilism of the early 1970s. Glam deliberately obfuscated the creative process, participating in its own estrangement. It rejected both the statutory dressing-down of rock and the earnest iconoclasm of the social turn in favour of an exuberant, and often vulgar, counter-reformation. Thus glam dandyism heralded a different account of the postmodern turn in British culture, one more familiar in the 1980s, and one that has been re-acknowledged more recently.[8]

Dressing up, rather than down, playing in the ruins, was another way of responding to Britain's dismal drift towards authoritarianism. The mannerist performances of the Nice Style: The World's First Pose Band and Gilbert & George at the turn of the 1970s can be seen as precedents in this regard. However, from a Po-Mo perspective, this work was too well respected by existing art institutions, too well articulated in its straight-breaks with late modernist art theory. The glam end of Po-Mo emerged from a less 'legitimate' place, one that was either ignored or deported by the art world border patrol in the early 1970s. Of course, for the glam generation who spent the 1950s as grammar school beatniks or secondary modern teen rebels, such borders were simply not there.

Friends say it's fine, friends say it's good
Ev'rybody says it's just like rock and roll.[9]

True to its theatrical proclivities, glam perpetually resurrected and killed off this paradise lost, the transmutation of the first frissons of 1950s teen rebellion into rock and roll. With rock and roll as its becoming-fetish, glam's sensual world was hewn from cheaply fabricated materials, a hub-cap diamond star halo of gold lamé, silver foil, vinyl, glitter, sequins, skintight jumpsuits, top hats, platform boots, make-up and mullets.[10] In the early 1970s, the artist Duggie Fields was developing a comparable chintzy repertoire of fifties-inspired pick'n'mix Po-Mo, one that integrated art, music, fashion and interior design. Fields has spent much of his life transforming his flat in Earl's Court Square, London, into a monument to the post-war glamour of 1950s *moderne*, an eclectic glam repertoire of plastics, vinyl leatherette, acrylic fibres, *tachisme*, 'pre-Adel Rootstein' mannequins and 'National Milk Bar' formica – just like rock and roll.[11] Like Nice Style: The World's First Pose Band, Fields cut straight to the chase with great prescience. The pop celebrity of the future would have no need to develop musical talent; gesture was everything. Ostentatious parties and overactive sartorial imaginations were the media through which Fields and his Chelsea Arts Club set communicated.[12] Field's kiss-curl all-over style was embodied best in his immaculate foppery, and in his frequent forays into fashion and interior design.

Very Fifth Avenue sixties psychedelic. The
Andrew Logan mirror glass palm tree at the
door must be the latest update on this line of
thinking.[13]

Andrew Logan's brush with the 'Haute Bo, Rich Hippie'[14] end of the counterculture came in 1967, when he worked in the United States and Canada for a year. His Alternative Miss World

Margaret Harrison
Banana Woman 1971
Graphite, pencil and watercolour on paper

Mick Rock
Andrew Logan as Alternative Miss World host / hostess 1973

Left: Andrew Logan and Derek Jarman, Downham Road studio
London, 1972

Left, below: Andrew Logan's Bedroom 1973

Opposite: Documentation from *The Alternative Miss World*:
Left to right, top to bottom: Miss Kitsch N Bitch (1973); Miss Holland
Park greets Miss Crêpe Suzette (1975); Miss Hackney (1975); Miss
Babylon (1975)

FILE

$3 AUTUMN 1975

GLAMOUR ISSUE

Opposite: FILE Megazine, 'Glamour Issue' (Vol. 3, No. 1, autumn 1975)
Web offset periodical, black and white reproductions and spot colour

Above: General Idea
The 1971 Miss General Idea Entry Kit 1971
Mixed media

Right: General Idea
Artist's Conception: Miss General Idea 1971
Screenprint on salmon wove paper

Artist's Conception; Miss General Idea 1971.

Competition[15] – a party inaugurated in 1972 in the run-up to London's first Gay Pride rally[16] – was, in part, a continuation of the counterculture's carnivalesque use of happenings, events, festivals and actions. The idea wasn't new, since the first pansexual Miss General Idea beauty pageant had been held at the St. Lawrence Centre for the Arts, Toronto, in August 1970.[17] In its transvestism, exhibitionism, affectation and performativity, and its nod to the decadence of Warhol's Factory, it shared the competition's glam vision. However, while the General Idea pageant was inspired by Marshall McLuhan's concept of a transmedia virus, the Alternative Miss World Competition harboured a less radicalised desire to indulge in unlimited intermediality.

Amateur hour goes on and on.[18]

First held at Logan's studio in Hackney, the competition soon became pivotal to the development of British Po-Mo, an annual opportunity to invent an extravagant and impetuous avatar, to become famous for being flamboyant. Against virtuosity, Logan's production values were a glam celebration of the discarded, the misshapen and the vernacular. Interviewed by his friend Derek Jarman in 1973,he revealed how he began raiding jumble sales in the early 1960s to develop his host-hostess outfits.[19] It's significant that Logan began practising as an architect in North America during the period in which architectural practice and theory were undergoing the first seeds of postmodern reform – a reformation licensed by bricolage.[20] His early installations, domestic grottos such as his indoor landscape in *Ten Sitting Rooms* (1970, ICA, London), were collaged together from plastic, bric-a-brac, cotton wool, broken mirrors, up-cycled furniture and decorative architectural salvage. Combined with Field's Earl's Court apartment, this set a precedent for a vein of Po-Mo that embraced fashion and interiors – both taboos in the deadly serious, macho-minimal world of late modernism. 'Ducks' rather than 'decorated sheds', these works suggested that he had learned something from Las Vegas. Logan's homespun assemblages produced an impressive celebration of wastefulness and non-normative masculinity, one echoed by the most celebrated glam acolytes to emerge, like Logan, from the flower-power hippiedom of the late 1960s: Marc Bolan, Brian Eno and David Bowie.

Social functionalism in the art of the 1970s (as in the 1990s) concerned the generation of zones that were continuous with the audience: a downstage, or plateau, that the artist can share with his or her followers. In some senses, this relational quest to (as Marc Bolan might have put it) 'bang the whole gang'[21] echoes rock's fantasy of revolutionary authenticity, its fixation with the profane, with merging into a common

denominator. The Alternative Miss World Competition promoted this fantasy of inclusivity in a different way, the audience invited to take to the catwalk to compete for 'best in show'. Everyone would become stylish and elegant together. Class, 'classiness', style, taste were, in Po-Mo, considered to be theatrical and mercurial, spreading something approaching glam rock's extraterrestrial remoteness and theatrical intensity. Against the grain of the times, this was an affirmative, upwardly mobile culture.

Alternative Miss World competitors were in an incomplete process of transformation – they were, at most, avatars. This was part of the appeal: the knowledge that the conservatism, ennui and stagflation of the early 1970s lay on the audience's side of the proscenium arch. Grandiose exhibitionism, gender-bending, entitlement exploitativeness... and yet it somehow seemed invisible, an intimate private party. At a time when it remained illegal for two people of the same sex to kiss in public, the counterculture was 'revolting into style.'[22]

While the whole spectrum of authority, from liberal academics to right-wing politicians, was fantasized into an oppressive establishment, there was very little unity within the underground, especially between the revolutionary Left and the counter-cultural hedonists.[23]

The counterculture's demands for wide-ranging political freedoms slowly transmogrified into a narrower, more individualised desire for the freedom to pursue pleasure. Self-fulfilment and freedom of choice were the hip-capitalist echoes of a re-emerging doctrine of neo-liberalism.[24] The Alternative Miss World was a certainly a political carnival, yet in comparison with the direct action pursued by the Gay Liberation Front it was a largely symbolic form of resistance, one very much aware of its limitations. Glam rock, similarly, offered the jouissance of teen rebellion as a highly theatrical break with the broader normative culture of the 'silent majority', but no more. As the 1970s rolled on, the reactionary backlash grew stronger.

As devastation mounted
My wardrobes almost burned
The teens held hands on shifting sands
And wonder what they learnt.[25]

Glam is not just another plastic art, one frozen in time as an 'authentic' object, a normative type for contemplation. It is, rather, a perpetually dynamic and perverse performance of style. In the twenty-first century, the bitter glitter of 1970s trashy glam has been usurped by an older, much more conservative, idea of glamour. Glamour has no past and no future. It has no cracks to paper over; it offers a hermetically sealed surface. Today everyone runs their own PR campaign of virtual preening, broadcasting narcissistic accounts of mundane events as if they signified a life of sovereign aestheticism. In contrast to glam, glamour is consumed with the pursuit of virtuosity, with the creation of airlessly immaculate effigies of the self. Glamour is consummately Photoshopped, it is never amateurish and it never acknowledges the fourth wall. Glamour is, to borrow Walter Scott's popularisation, unadulterated magic, enchantment personified. Glamour tries too hard. While glam might ultimately have been complicit with the hip capitalism that followed in the wake of the 1960s counterculture, it did at least offer the apparent prospect of rebellion. It offered ordinary kids the rapturous illusion of an exit from an increasingly grim present. Glamour, in contrast, offers no way in, and no way out.

1 Sparks, 'Talent is an Asset', *Kimono My House*, Island LP, 1974.
2 The title of an exhibition at the Hayward Gallery, London, 1972.
3 This position was widely popularised by John Berger's *Ways of Seeing* TV series, which launched on 8 January 1972.
4 Unemployment passed one million in January 1972 for the first time in over thirty years.
5 See John A. Walker's *Left Shift: Radical Art in 1970s Britain*, London: IB Taurus, 2002.
6 Lars Bang Larsen, 'The Long Nineties', *Frieze*, 44, January–February 2012, pp. 92–5.
7 For example, Matthew Higgs and Paul Noble's *Protest and Survive* (Whitechapel, London, 2000–2001) made explicit the political connections between the socially engaged art of the 1990s and the social functionalism in art of the early 1970s. Our understanding of art in 1970s Britain is therefore filtered through our continued immersion in 1990s approaches to art practice.
8 The V&A's exhibition *Postmodernism: Style and Subversion 1970-1990* (24 September 2011 to 15 January 2012) is a case in point, taking its lead from Robert Venturi, Denise Scott Brown and Charles Jencks' 'co-opted' postmodernism-as-style (hyphenated to indicate Jencks' formulation: 'Po-Mo') at the expense of the more politically charged 'critical postmodern-ist' project that we might indentify in the *New Art*.
9 T. Rex, '20th Century Boy', EMI 7" single, 1973.
10 T. Rex, 'Get it On', *Electric Warrior*, EMI LP, 1971.
11 Peter York, 'Them', in *Style Wars*, London: Sidgwick & Jackson, 1980, p. 126.
12 In particular, Zandra Rhodes, the Logan brothers and Dick Jewell.
13 Peter York, 'Bowie Night', in *Style Wars*, p. 241.
14 Ibid.
15 Downham Road Studio, Hackney, London, 25 March 1972.
16 Organised by the Gay Liberation Front, the rally marched from Trafalgar Square to Hyde Park, London, on 1 July 1972. The Pride march is now an annual event. The march formed a counterpoint to the reactionary 'Nationwide Festival of Light' held in Hyde Park and Trafalgar Square in September 1971.
17 General Idea published a 'Glamour Issue' of their maga-zine *FILE* in Autumn 1975.
18 Sparks, 'Amateur Hour', on *Kimono My House*, Island LP, 1974.
19 See 'Andrew Logan interviewed by Derek Jarman', *Inter-view*, April 1973.
20 Robert Venturi, Denise Scott Brown and Steven Izenour, *A Significance for A&P Parking Lots, or Learning from Las Vegas*, published in 1968 by *Architectural Forum*, signifies the shift towards the postmodern embrace of a rich heritage of iconog-raphy and allegory and its attitude of amused, agnostic pragmatism.
21 T. Rex, 'Baby Boomerang', B-side of 'I Love to Boogie', EMI 7" single, 1976.
22 See George Melly, *Revolt into Style: The Pop Arts in Britain*, London: Allen Lane, 1970.
23 Robert Hewison, *Too Much: Art and Society in the Sixties 1960–1975*, London: Methuen, 1986, p. 154.
24 I'm thinking here of neoliberal economics such as the 1969 'Selsdon Park Hotel' monetarist policies with which the Conservatives won the 1970 general election and the 'shock therapy' aggressively pursued by the IMF in the 1970s. The development of Po-Mo accompanies the beginning of the breakdown of the postwar 'Keynesian consensus', radical changes to how 'mixed' capitalist economies were admin-istered. Notably, Daniel Bell's *The Coming of Post-Industrial Society: A Venture in Social Forecasting* was published in 1973. The split with Keynesianism was short-lived, as Edward Heath quickly abandoned monetarism, but it remained the great unfinished ideological business of the New Right. See Kevin Hickson, *The IMF Crisis of 1976 and British Politics: Keynesian Social Democracy, Monetarism and Economic Liberalism: The 1970s Struggle in British Politics*, London: IB Taurus, 2005.
25 T. Rex, 'Teen Riot Structure', on *Dandy of the Underworld*, EMI LP, 1977.

Crocodile Tears: A Counter-Archive of Glam Aesthetics

Dominic Johnson

'Like Pandora's box,' writes the artist Catherine Lord, 'no archive is opened without an intention to reconfigure and re-inscribe, which is to say, to propose and [...] institute a counter-archive.'[1] Such a 'counter-archive' – whose unruliness is suggested by Lord's simile – is perhaps instantiated by devoting critical energies to the parallels between 'glam' culture and visual art, in the 1970s and after.

'Glam' is a nebulous, contentious term, embracing music, fashion, culture and art. It is signified in general terms by aesthetic overstatement: androgyny, gender fuck, psychedelia, glitter and rhinestone make-up, metallic polyester and bright vinyl clothing, feather boas, big hair and platform boots. For Dave Thompson, glam bleeds into similarly fringe styles such as 'bubblegum, or pub rock, or belated psych-pop, or proto-punk, or any of the myriad other genres we now declare

Jack Smith
Untitled c.1958–62/2011
C-print on paper

Steven Arnold
Connecting to the Infinite 1987
Silver gelatin print

were burgeoning', especially between 1971 and 1975, when glam was predominantly active.[2] Crucially, glam is an indeterminate genre – historically, culturally, and in terms of which figures can and cannot be included in its scope. Glam is therefore less a discrete form than 'an attitude, a feeling, a shift in societal tempo and an upsurge in cultural awareness', Thomson writes.[3] Glam's hybridity and indeterminacy, its central resistance to definitive classification, make it an apposite term for resignifying a broader range of artistic practices – that is, towards a 'counter-archive' of late-twentieth-century art.

A glam counter-archive would include subcultural practices in recent visual culture, for example the gaudy filmic dream worlds of Steven Arnold, James Bidgood, Jack Smith, or George Kuchar; the drag pageantry of performances by BLOOLIPS or the Cockettes; the effete theatricality of dances by Lindsay Kemp or Michael Clark; the oddball polka-dot contagion of Yayoi Kusama's sculptures; or the uncanny Technicolor haze of Jimmy De Sana's photographs. I focus on the work of Steven Arnold here, with reference to other artists. Arnold particularly retains the subcultural flair of glitter, glamour, poetry and magic, yet his representations of nudity often restyle the sexual ambivalence that glam rock required to secure its superstars' commercial viability. Like glam, he also refuses the determinacy of meaning, glamourising the confusions that gleam from surface qualities. Glam is seemingly unabashed in privileging 'style over substance', a phrase often tinged with disparagement yet celebrated (even if passively) by its superstars. Listening to Marc Bolan's voice, for example, I am seduced by the inverse profundity of lines such as 'Baby you're a champ, but / Girl you ain't nothing but a raw ramp' (from 'Raw Ramp', B-side of T. Rex's single 'Get It On' of 1971), which suggest a voluptuous (but anodyne) sexuality, yet remain conceptually ambivalent. How might Bolan's strategic vacuity be transposed to similarly glittering emptiness in the visual work of artists in the same period? Glam seems to rebuke the myth of a residual truth or stable meaning at the supposedly numinous heart of a work. This refusal of hermeneutic closure is appropriated, intensified and theatricalised in the work of Steven Arnold and others.

In *Performing Glam Rock* (2006), Philip Auslander appropriates glam as a case study for theorising identity, gender and sexuality. For Auslander, glam is 'not so much a musicological category as a sociological one.'[4] He defines the adoption of feminised, queered and spectacular aesthetics as 'post-countercultural' in order to explain glam's apparent departure from the earlier 'guerrilla' and agitprop politics of the late 1950s and 1960s, in which the cultural vanguards – from

Jimmy De Sana
Marker Cones 1982
Silver dye bleach print

Jimmy De Sana
Pool 1980
Silver dye bleach print

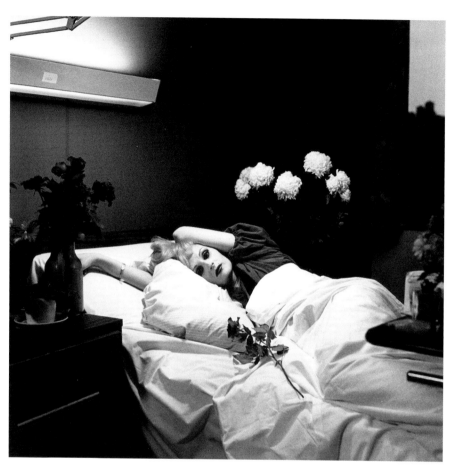

Above: Peter Hujar
Sweet Pam (Cockette) 1973
Silver gelatin print

Right: Peter Hujar
Candy Darling on her Deathbed 1973
Silver gelatin print

Below, left to right: Peter Hujar
Jackie Curtis and Lance Loud 1975
Silver gelatin print

Peter Hujar
Fayette 1973
Silver gelatin print

Peter Hujar
Stephen Varble, Soho, Franklin Street
1976
Silver gelatin print

Opposite: Peter Hujar
John Rothermell in a Fashion Pose 1973
Silver gelatin print

Beats to Black Panthers, Valerie Solanas to Shulamith Firestone, hippies to Yippies – were fixated upon authenticity, essence, spontaneity, depth, and the smashing of consumer-oriented 'false consciousness'. Sartorial excess, stage antics, and other visual eccentricities of glam were 'clearly a *theatrical* gesture in conflict with a counterculture that was ambivalent, at best, [towards] theatricality.'[5] While both upheld the importance of play, outrage and cryptic singularity, glam can be seen to celebrate irony, fakery, opacity and glamour, in contrast to the countercultural values of sincerity, verisimilitude, transparency and the communion with nature. As the proto-glam artist and filmmaker Jack Smith – himself no stranger to fairy queen aesthetics – writes, the sincerity of the counterculture could be unfixed by a personal commitment to 'Glamourous Rapture, schizophrenic delight, hopeless naiveté, and glittering technicolor trash!'[6]

Born in Berkeley, California in 1943, Arnold is a crucial figure for a glam counter-archive. In his late teens, he left the well-to-do social environs in which he was raised (his mother was a noted illustrator and fashion designer), and enrolled in the MFA programme at the San Francisco Art Institute. Upon graduating, he left the United States in 1964 for a brief sojourn in Paris, where he enrolled in the École des Beaux-Arts. Frustrated by its pedagogical approach, he returned to San Francisco via Barcelona and Tangier, picking up new esoteric influences along the way, and settled again in the Mission district until the late 1970s.[7] The grand achievement of his time in San Francisco was his film *Luminous Procuress* (1971), discussed in more detail below. In 1979, Arnold left San Francisco for Los Angeles, with the ambition of making feature films in Hollywood, but his outlandish aesthetics ensured him more marginal spaces of production, and he eventually abandoned filmmaking for photography.[8] He lived in Los Angeles until his untimely death from an AIDS-related illness on 6 August 1994, aged 51.

Arnold's photography set a precedent for more commercially viable artists such as David LaChapelle and Pierre et Gilles. His work revels in surface qualities and his sitters' apparently narcissistic self-regard, and honours the cheap charm of decorative detritus into which they look plunged or set adrift. Arnold's images are strikingly ornamental and depthless, couched in the terms of West Coast mysticism and Jungian archetypes. In them Arnold creates, in Ed Halter's striking description, 'lysergic fantasy worlds from meagre means.'[9] Arnold's signature method involved sketching his dreams in linear drawings that resemble those of Jean Cocteau. Using these fantastical images as storyboards, he built elaborate sets in his studio for the ensuing tableaux. Arnold often arranged the

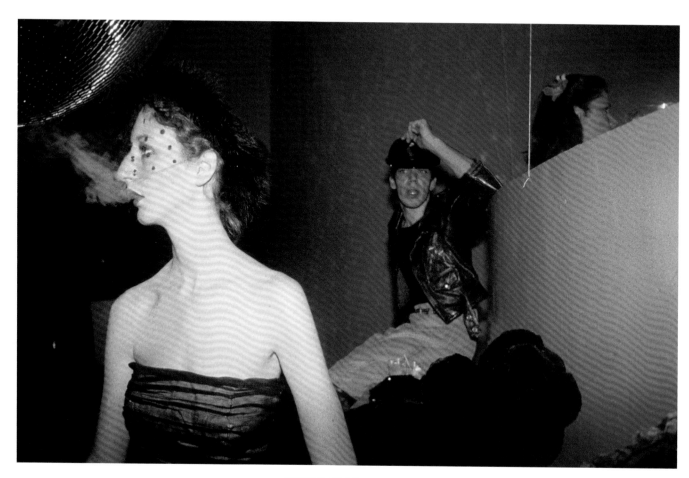

Above: Nan Goldin
Naomi and Marlene on the balcony, Boston 1972
Gelatin silver print

Right: Nan Goldin
Kenny putting on make-up, Boston 1973
Cibachrome print

Opposite, top: Nan Goldin
Robin and Kenny, Boston 1978
Cibachrome print

Opposite, bottom: Nan Goldin
Christmas at the Other Side, Boston 1972
Gelatin silver print

adorned bodies, furniture and props on a stage, and shot them squarely from the front. Less frequently, they were laid out in a busy field on the floor, and photographed from above by Arnold hanging on a trapeze installed in the centre of the studio, which produced, in photographs such as *Heal-a-zation Swathe à la Glob Ba* (1981), the disconcerting effect of subjects floating in a sea of glittering objects and fabric. Arnold lit his scenes with tungsten lamps to create striking chiaroscuro, and used a Hasselblad 500C medium-format camera and Tri-X film. He neither cropped nor retouched his negatives, and made bold, square, glossy black-and-white prints mounted on white matting board. Arnold's studio in Los Angeles – a renovated pretzel factory that he renamed Zanzabar (after a long-forgotten circus clown) – was a collecting place for friends and celebrities, decorated according to a personal taste he described as 'Barnum and Bailey fucks Louis the fourteenth, in drag.'[10] A retinue of figures populates his images, often returning in new costumes and make-up throughout his oeuvre, and in colour in earlier works such as *Luminous Procuress*.

Salvador Dalí was an influential friend and supporter. In 1973, Arnold was in New York for a screening of *Luminous Procuress* at the Whitney Museum of American Art when his friend Kaisik Wong, the pioneer of wearable art, introduced him to Dalí, who held open court for the glitterati at the St. Regis Hotel. Dalí was struck by the mystical excess of *Luminous Procuress*, and by Arnold's eccentric personal style and charisma. Arnold joined the ageing artist's retinue, 'the Court of Miracles' – as Dalí's 'Prince' – alongside other fringe icons: transsexual pop star Amanda Lear; the first black supermodel Donyale Luna; Ultra Violet and other 'superstars' on sabbatical from Andy Warhol's Factory; and rock musicians such as David Bowie, Mick Jagger and Marianne Faithfull. Crucially, Arnold assisted Dalí with final preparations for the opening of his Teatro-Museo Dalí in Figueres, Spain in 1974. He attended the opening with Wong, Pandora (Arnold's childhood friend, muse, and the star of *Luminous Procuress*) and Merle Bulatao, each kitted out in extravagant ceremonial costumes by Wong. 'They looked as if they had all stepped out of a Chinese folk-tale and Dalí found them inoffensively magnificent', Amanda Lear recalled in her gossipy memoir of the 'Court of Miracles'.[11]

Dalí had a profound effect on Arnold, influencing his outward appearance as a starry-eyed eccentric, as well as the styling of his own photos and drawings. Arnold described his 'apprenticeship' with Dalí as '[one] great déjà vu re-echoing the childhood vision of my own destiny.'[12] In his ambivalence and ostentatious superficiality, Dalí is a suggestive

Opposite: Ray Johnson
Untitled (Frank O'Hara) 1973
Collage on board

Opposite, below: Ray Johnson
Untitled (Cupid with Jackie Curtis Saluting) 1974
Collage on board

Below: Ray Johnson
Untitled (Toothbrush with David Bowie) 1979-87-88-90-91+
Collage on board

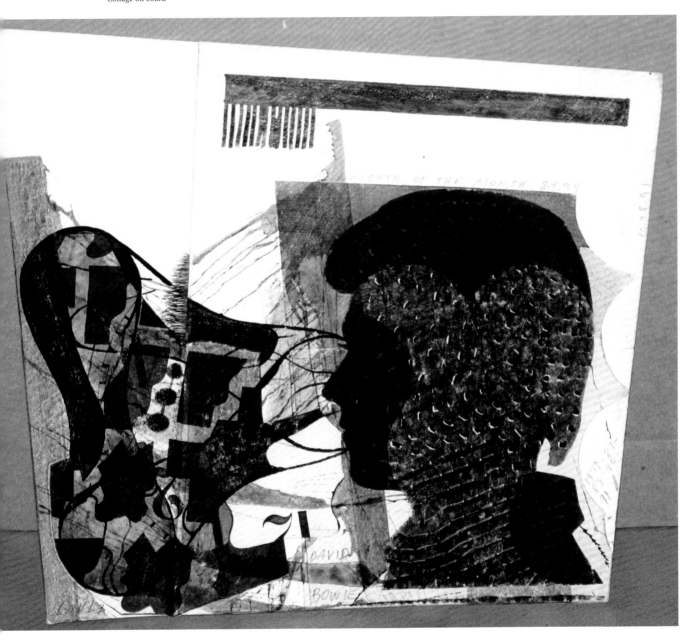

precursor to the counter-archive of glam art and culture more generally. Indeed, in the year he met Arnold, glam culture directly inspired Dalí to create *First Cylindric Chrono-Hologram Portrait of Alice Cooper's Brain* 1973, one of two technologically advanced 3D white light integral holographic portraits. The multi-coloured work features a projection of the seated glam shock-rocker Cooper biting a statuette of the Venus de Milo, naked but for a diamond tiara and necklace designed by Dalí for Harry Winston.

Through his own glam circle of 'angels of night', Arnold translated Dalí's 'nuclear' Surrealism into West Coast psychedelic mysticism, and developed his own style by combining elements of classicism and an ambitious junk art aesthetic. *Luminous Procuress* introduced Arnold's human flotsam to a wider audience. In the film's meagre narrative, Pandora, the 'procuress' of Arnold's title, telepathically lures two men into a grand house. Installed in an extravagant attic boudoir, Pandora displays an aquiline nose, high forehead, soft pink Regency wig, and ice-cool demeanour. Scored to sounds of interplanetary communications, antic strings and unintelligible murmurs, her courtiers laze in posing pouches, indulging in blithe chatter. Pandora procures her boys through a drawn-out mystical staring contest, which segues into a performance by the Cockettes, the drag troupe that dominated San Francisco's Haight-Ashbury scene between 1970 and 1973, and who were fixtures at Arnold's midnight movie screenings at the Palace Theatre. In 1971, during an ill-fated tour to New York's Anderson Theatre, Peter Hujar photographed the Cockettes, depicting the group in a series of striking portraits that capture their cheap glamour and seductive superficiality. In *Luminous Procuress*, the Cockettes appear on a proscenium stage, and wave feathers, tulle, beaded trains and genitalia, accompanied by a monkey organ grinder. The procured couple watch the proceedings, sequestered in the shadows.

A fisheye lens augments the film's most luminous scenes, as Arnold pans across the entwined bodies of the Cockettes, gliding over their painted faces, lithe torsos and engorged sexes. The passage of his eye across bodies clearly recalls similar black-and-white scenes towards the beginning of Jack Smith's iconic underground film *Flaming Creatures* (1963). In Arnold's film, the entangled flesh is a backdrop for a superimposed red circle in which Pandora writhes, draped in a diaphanous veil. The couple wander through Pandora's underworld, coming across mystifying scenes of beauty, including Ruth Weiss studded in mirrors, raising and lowering a shiny metal sphere. In a *tableau vivant* by the Cockettes, Hibiscus appears wearing a grass skirt, pineapples for breasts, and a basket of fruit in his hair. The imagery is hallucinatory, tinged with magic, and

Below and opposite: Steven Arnold
Luminess Procuress 1971
DVD, colour, sound
Duration: 74 minutes

confounding. Of his work Arnold wrote: 'I like to glop up the space so that the viewer has to exercise his eye. If all goes well [...] his psyche gets taken for a ride too.'[13]

Arnold's work is a *tour de force* of style over substance, drawing in viewers to confound the straightforward production of meaning. Committing himself to photography several years after moving to Los Angeles – his earliest photographs of note are dated 1981 – Arnold's photos exceed the stylised fabulation of his films. *Connecting to the Infinite* 1987 is a characteristic photograph, published in Arnold's second book, *Epiphanies* of 1989. Centred in the frame, an athletic body stands on a stage, against a frenetic backdrop of white shapes mounted on a black screen. Cut-out circles, swirls, stars and flames emanate in febrile curlicues from his head, heart and outstretched arms. The image is a love poem to the marble heat of human flesh. Posed in the nethermost depths of an insomniac duration, the crowned figure is majestically unreadable. In his isolation, he suggests antique conjugal rites, spermatozoic projections, or the loss of identity in the astronomical swirl of an unidentified solstice. The details are seductive: the figure's eyes closed above burnished triangular tears, circles drawn around his nipples, a flaming codpiece, twinkling stigmata on his palms, and the painted marks pulsing down his legs and feet. *Connecting to the Infinite* is a triumph of fakery and theatricality. 'And in this meeting – call it an epiphany – something is healed,' Arnold wrote. 'I don't know what. Perhaps some wound that is common to us all.'[14] Rather than suggesting corporeal wounds, such 'heal-a-zation' – Arnold's neologism – instead suggests feeling adrift in a world of glamourous dissimulations, or otherwise being out of sync with oneself.

The affective charge that issues from a counter-archive of glam aesthetics is beatifically false, and shamelessly grandiose. Our emotions here are guileful ones – crocodile tears – the crystalline effects of beatific joy and idle dreaming.

1 Catherine Lord, 'Their Memory is Playing Tricks on Her: Notes Toward a Calligraphy of Rage', in Cornelia Butler, ed., *WACK! Art and the Feminist Revolution*, exh. cat., Museum of Contemporary Art, Los Angeles, Cambridge and London: MIT Press, 2007, pp. 441–57 (p. 441).
2 Dave Thompson, *Children of the Revolution: The Glam Rock Story, 1970–75*, London: Cherry Red Books, 2010, p. 5.
3 Ibid., p. 24.
4 Philip Auslander, *Performing Glam Rock: Gender and Theatricality in Popular Music*, Ann Arbor: University of Michigan Press, 2006, p. 50.
5 Ibid., p. 10. Emphasis in original.
6 Jack Smith, 'The Perfect Filmic Appositeness of Maria Montez', in J. Hoberman and Edward Leffingwell, eds., *Wait for Me at the Bottom of the Pool: The Writings of Jack Smith*, New York and London: High Risk Books, 1997, p. 26.
7 For recollections of Arnold's time in San Francisco, as a friend of the Cockettes, host of the Palace Theatre, and one of 'the original New Age luminaries', see 'Sweet' Pam Tent, *Midnight at the Palace: My Life as a Fabulous Cockette*, Los Angeles: Alyson Books, 2004, pp. 27–32.
8 Arnold published three books of photographs during his lifetime: *Reliquaries* 1983, *Epiphanies* 1989, and *Angels of Night* 1990, and participated in numerous exhibitions throughout the United States. A large collection of many of his best works was also published posthumously as *Exotic Tableaux* 1996.
9 Ed Halter, 'Dead Flowers', in Lia Gangitano, ed., *Dead Flowers*, exh. cat., Participant Inc, New York: Participant Press, 2011, pp. 258–63 (p. 259).
10 Peter Weiermair, 'Steven Arnold: A West Coast Eccentric – Remarks on his Staged Photography', in Steven Arnold: *Exotic Tableaux*, Frankfurt: Edition Stemmle, 1996, pp. 7–13 (p. 10).
11 Amanda Lear, *My Life with Dalí*, London: Virgin, 1985, p. 251.
12 Cited in James Leo Herlihy, 'Afterword', in *Steven Arnold: Epiphanies*, Pasadena: Twelvetrees Press, 1989, n. p.
13 Ibid.
14 Ibid.

Jack Smith
Untitled c.1958-1962/2011
C-prints on paper

Richard Hamilton, Art, Style, Personae and New Aesthetics

Michael Bracewell

Looking back on his time at Newcastle University in the mid-1960s, studying in the Department of Fine Art during the period when Richard Hamilton – as much a modern muse as a tutor – was in residence, the designer Nick de Ville (later designer by appointment to fellow student Bryan Ferry's art rock band, Roxy Music) would remark that there had been something in the air about art being made in the medium of assuming a persona.[1]

Hamilton himself, the great artist-intellectual, fervent Duchampian, pioneer analyst of the relationships between mass culture, technology, design and fine art, would not perhaps have expressed the situation in those terms – but the statement would still add up, along the continuum of Hamiltonian thinking. As befitted his creation of the Basic Course for first-year students, Hamilton was concerned with the pursuit of technical and creative lucidity, in a manner that might be

Richard Hamilton
Swingeing London 67 (f) 1968-9
Acrylic paint, screenprint, paper, aluminium and metalised acetate on canvas

developed, exponentially, across artistic processes to open up new and singular forms that art might take. His establishment of a course entitled 'The Found Image', for example, which prompted star pupil Mark Lancaster to repurpose the panels of a Maxwell House instant coffee advertisement as an artwork, opened up the studio to all the acceleration, glamour, wit, sexiness, weirdness and poised allure of 'popular culture'. But, in the spirit of Duchamp, Hamilton was less interested in prescribing a method of artistically responding to this second-hand material than in encouraging an intellectual and conceptual agility with which to explore the ways in which art might be made. Art made in the medium of creating a 'persona' – the ultimate rock and roll star, for example – might be just one option, and there would be others. But a robust bridge between 'popular' and 'classical' culture (or fine art) had been established.

Hamilton's art, ideas and writings were never in the thrall of mere intellectualism. As a worker-technician he made it his business to acquire a precise knowledge of whatever technical processes a project might demand. Likewise, those students who followed his ideas would be expected to think and work in technical terms – not dissimilar, perhaps, to acquiring the panoramic artisan-technical skills of Hollywood or car design, and routing such skills through fine art. Hence, in 1966, Hamilton's recreation of Duchamp's *Large Glass* would be – at least on the top level of the project – a primarily technical exercise, employing the range of drawing skills that he had learned as a student at the Royal Academy schools. He would subsequently remark that he could not find an assistant among his own students who was up to the task.

Precise technical knowledge and skill, therefore, were on Hamilton's curriculum – thus proposing both a conceptual-analytical and a mechanical understanding of art, process and mass culture. This was not an arid endeavour, but a new aesthetics. 'For I was after beauty, too', Hamilton would later affirm, as though this had not been clear all along, in the beguiling perfection of the way in which his art, across media, so seamlessly and eloquently fused the cool precision of design and technology with the erotic warmth of intense romanticism.[2] Hamilton wrote about Pop as the new world condition, which he approached with 'a mixture of reverence and cynicism that I would once have labelled "non-Aristotelian" but now prefer to call "cool."'[3]

Reviewing his long and distinguished career, Hamilton explained that he had never understood when Frank Stella said that he wanted to create an art that was 'non-allusive' – an art that referred solely to its own identity and rules. Hamilton,

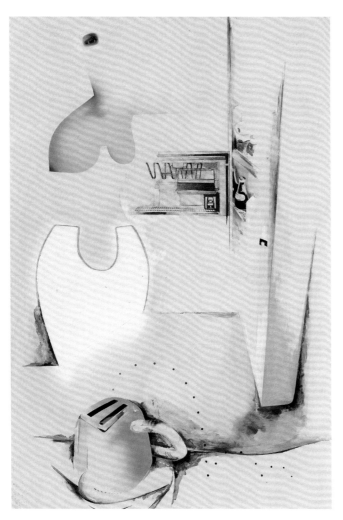

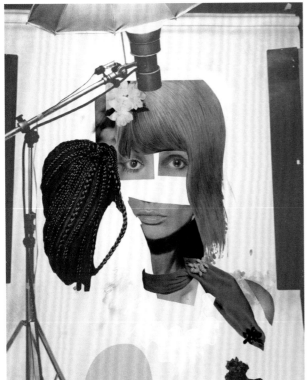

Above: Richard Hamilton and Robert Freeman
Self Portrait, cover of *Living Arts* 2 1963

Left: Richard Hamilton
Fashion Plate 1969/73
Photocollage, silkscreen, acrylic, cosmetic pencils and glitter on paper

Opposite: Richard Hamilton
$he 1958-61
Oil, cellulose paint and collage on wood

by contrast, wanted his art to be 'multi-allusive' – referring out to the whole world, in all of its modern layers and processes of thought and industry and feeling and politics.[4]

Such an ambition, perhaps, prompted David Sylvester's subsequent description of Hamilton as an artist resolutely committed *not* to 'Pop' (with which he was mainly identified) but to the 'modern' – and 'modern' in a specific cultural and art-historical sense. In their profound relationship to the art and ideas of Marcel Duchamp (regarded in the mid-1960s, according to another Newcastle graduate, Tim Head, as 'either the Saviour or Anti-Christ of art'[5]), Hamilton's own activities had their ancestry in Surrealism and Dada – while being in no way Surrealist nor in the belated service of Dada.

For Hamilton, the notion of the 'modern' (which a contemporary such as Bridget Riley would see as a descendant, artistically, intellectually and spiritually, of Impressionism and Post-Impressionism) clearly had its origins in a point of conceptualist iconoclasm at the beginning of the twentieth century: a grand abandoning of art's 'rules' in favour of an art that was indeed 'multi-allusive', in accordance with its own ideals, and open to any and all media – as long as those media could be justified artistically and intellectually. This was the modern world, and the old rules no longer applied in quite the same way. Such a divergence of attitudes would create an irreconcilable schism in British art during the mid-twentieth century and later. By the late 1960s, in the British art schools and university departments of fine art, this schism would polarise staff and students, while being assimilated into the then fashionable, some would argue pressing, political concerns of the counterculture – to dismantle as a point of principle any semblance of conditioning authority.

As Baudelaire had predicted some hundred and twenty years earlier, in his writings on dandyism within his series of essays 'The Painter of Modern Life' (1863), precisely such times of upheaval create the perfect conditions under which a certain kind of artist – an artist whose media might indeed include lifestyle, or the meticulous construction of a 'persona' – can operate. To wit:

Dandyism appears especially in those periods of transition when democracy has not yet become all-powerful, and when aristocracy is only partially weakened and discredited. In the confusion of such times, a certain number of men, disenchanted and leisured 'outsiders', but all of them richly endowed with native energy, may conceive the idea of establishing a new kind of aristocracy, all the more difficult to break down because established on the most precious, the most

Roxy Music
Roxy Music 1972
(LP, Island Records)

Roxy Music
Inner sleeve of *For Your Pleasure* 1973
(LP, Island Records)

Opposite: Margaret Harrison
Take One Lemon 1971
Lithograph on paper

indestructible faculties, on the divine gifts that neither work nor money can give. Dandyism is the last flicker of heroism in decadent ages...[6]

Hamilton's own dandyism – white Levi's, cigar and a silk neckerchief – was secondary; Duchamp's version was more a cloak of invisibility (indeed, the point of the dandy, in Baudelaire's founding theology, was to dress with such 'correctness' that one became invisible.) But under a railway arch in east London, two young students from Saint Martins School of Art were appearing in neat, ordinary suits and ties, their faces painted gold, to create a 'living sculpture' that was based on an old music-hall song called 'Underneath the Arches'. They sang in fine clear voices and moved robotically, standing on a table placed some way behind a length of string, which marked the boundary within which the sculpture existed. Photographs of the occasion show, in the scant audience, Richard Hamilton and his partner, artist Rita Donagh.

Gilbert & George first blurred and then evaporated the (already very) fine line between their pre-living sculpture selves and the notion of art made in the medium of persona. Shortly after they met, Gilbert & George had had the revelation that they were their art, and that their lives together, as living sculptures, were inseparable from this art. Walking, eating, drinking, dancing, writing, drawing – all were equal parts of the total artwork created by their partnership. Art-historically, Gilbert & George were independent of any lineage or tradition or 'school' or movement; rather, their art reversed every creative, intellectual, political and ideological tenet commonly attributed to modern and contemporary art.

As living sculptures they espoused above all direct communication – an art of feelings and emotions, as opposed to concepts, atelier skills and ideas. Likewise they repudiated with equal force any assimilation into the causes of Fluxus, Pop and the austere finesse of minimalism and the cause of abstraction (in particular, any school of art devolving from Continental Europe) and asserted instead, in their lives-as-art, the opposite of all prevailing trends: they dressed soberly, with neat, clerical haircuts, as opposed to informally or 'fashionably'. They used the idiom of formal or even ceremonial politeness, rejecting at root the rhetoric of the counterculture or the avant-garde.

Their tastes enriched the auto-faction of 'the world of Gilbert & George'. The only artists they liked, for example, were English visionaries, pre-Raphaelites and mid-Victorian architects, potters and designers - then anathema to 'educated' taste. All was reversed, in the art of Gilbert & George. By means as resolute and unyielding as they were fundamentally simple, they created what could be called an immaculate tension in their art, whereby their very conservatism of style rendered their work shocking, violent, original – its intentionality at once ambiguous, deeply felt, anarchically libertarian and profoundly poetic.

During the latter half of the 1960s, from a deepening confluence of fine artistic and mass cultural ideas, a new aestheticism became possible within the interface between fine art and the burgeoning world of a Pop-era lifestyle. The glamour of mass-cultural Americana; the poise, charm and melancholy of a remembered or fantastical Edwardian and imperial England; dandyism and games with stylistic time travel – all would play their roles within this new art/Pop sensibility.

There had been some earlier hints at such a fusion of 'art' ideas and 'Pop' awareness. Within the art schools, for example, immediately following the vogue for 'Trad Jazz' – as typified by Chris Barber and his band – in the late 1950s, there had been a student/rag enthusiasm for a form of English Dada, in which stylistic games played out with Victoriana, music hall, the jazz bands and 'novelty songs' of the 1920s were rolled into a volatile and slapstick form of musical performance, exemplified first by the The Alberts and later – achieving considerable mainstream success, and contributing to the rich seam of British comedy from which 'Monty Python's Flying Circus' would emerge – and as featured in The Beatles' ill-feted television film of 1967 'The Magical Mystery Tour', the Bonzo Dog Doo-Dah Band.

The concern of such 'Pop' activities with pose, comedy and games with the history of style – in particular the notion of formality and archaic Englishness, and the transmission, beneath the surface of studied politeness and quaintness, of evident intellectual or artistic mischief-making – might be seen to contribute a further strand to the new aesthetics of pose and persona which would connect the ideas of Pop to the capacities of fine art during the late 1960s and 1970s. Nice Style's 'High Up on a Baroque Palazzo' performance of 1974, for example, might be seen to continue the lineage in a cooler and sharper vein; while Brian Eno, speaking about the creation of Roxy Music – arguably the house band of the new aesthetics – would propose that the group members saw themselves 'as a school of art set up in opposition to all prevailing trends', while assuming a new form of dandyism and 'male beauty', in which their chosen garb (immediately picked up by their vast audience) suggested a self-projection as 'Masters of the Intergalactic Parliament'.[7]

In October 1976, the journalist and trend analyst Peter York (himself in fact the created persona of one Peter Wallis, a management consultant) published an essay in

Richard Hamilton
Soft Pink Landscape 1971-2
Oil on canvas

Above: Peter Schlesinger
Amanda Lear, Colville Terrace c.1970
C-print on paper

Right: Peter Schlesinger
Gala Mitchell, Colville Terrace c.1970
C-print on paper

Opposite, top: Peter Schlesinger
David Hockney and Cecil Beaton, Reddish House 1970
C-print on paper

Opposite, left: Peter Schlesinger
Manalo Blahnik, Colville Terrace 1972
C-print on paper

Previous pages and above:
Marc Camille Chaimowicz
Celebration? Realife 1972-2000
Mixed media

Harpers & Queen magazine in his capacity as the publication's 'Style Editor'. Titled 'Them', this essay nailed – as far as anyone was likely to – the cumulative consequences of the new school of aesthetics that had emerged, refracting ideas born in art schools through fashion, design and pop music, to be taken up within the medium of 'lifestyle' – an *art-directed* lifestyle, in which art might take the form of assuming a persona, or creating an environment (domestic or retail/commercial) that might both resemble and assume the function of a film set.[8]

York was less concerned with recent art history than with identifying a style trend in which the ideas behind Pop art or the deployment of glamour and camp as a form of high aesthetic iconoclasm were put into the service of a lifestyle dedicated entirely to art and style. The followers of this fashion he dubbed 'Them'. One might borrow from Jean Cocteau (a 'Them' figure, if ever there was one), writing in 1934, to summarise the anthropology of this new style tribe:

Our gang wasn't really one. It grew more numerous by a gyratory phenomenon of molecular affinities, a kind of internal style. But it remained inaccessible to those who pulled strings in order to become part of it.[9]

Once again, the suggestion of an exclusive 'style aristocracy', emerging to make new associations and create new strategies within the language of art, is linked with the idea of oppositional aesthetics: the use of connoisseurship and art-historical research, coupled with technical artisanal skills, as the basis of a new form of art-making (exemplified in contemporary terms by the work of both Marc Camille Chaimowicz and Lucy McKenzie) in which the 'total art work' comprises the habitat, accoutrements and very consciousness of a chosen or adopted persona, from their bed to the books they might read and the lamps they might read them by. The artist thus becomes part Vicomtesse Marie-Laure de Noailles, curating a total lifestyle of amplified modernism, and part dedicated craftsperson, painstakingly acquiring the technical skills required to construct that persona's magic kingdom. Whether the acquisition of these skills is also a further part of the performed self of a persona remains of necessity open to conjecture.

1 Research interview with the author for *Re-make/Re-model: Art, Pop, Fashion and the making of Roxy Music, 1953 – 1972*, London: Faber & Faber, London, 2006.
2 Interview with the author, Northend Farm, Oxford, April 2007.
3 *Richard Hamilton, Collected Words*, London: Thames & Hudson, 1983.
4 Interview with the author, Northend Farm, Oxford, April 2007.
5 Research interview with the author for *Re-make/Re-model*, op. cit.
6 Charles Baudelaire, 'The Painter of Modern Life' (1863), in *Charles Baudelaire: Life and Other Essays*, Jonathan Mayne, trans., London: Phaidon, 2006.
7 Research interview with Brian Eno conducted for *Re-make/Re-model*, op. cit.
8 Peter York, 'Them', *Harpers & Queen*, October 1976, pp. 204-209.
9 Jean Cocteau quoted in Philip Core, *The Original Eye: Arbiters of Twentieth Century Taste*, New Jersey: Prentice Hall, 1984, p. 121.

The Birth of Glitter Rock

Glenn O'Brien

Glam happened in the Atlantic Ocean, halfway between London New York. In the 1960s designer Mary Quant invented the miniskirt in London. Meanwhile in New York designer Vicky Tiel invented the miniskirt. That's the way it works. Ideas whose time have come are in the air for those with the vision to catch them. Take glam... it came from London, it came from New York. It came from the sky. It was synchronicity – the only thing that could possibly follow the 1960s hippie era.

When I arrived in New York City in 1970, even though virtually all the major record labels were headquartered here, it was probably the worst city in the world in which to secure a record contract. Jimi Hendrix had to leave New York for London to get famous. (He was so glam before Glam!) The Velvet Underground were a flop at home. The summer I arrived they played Max's Kansas City, and then Lou quit the group and moved in with his parents. Their last performance was recorded on a

Billy Sullivan
Jackie Curtis, West 87th Street, New York 1969

Anton Perich
Andrea Feldman outside Max's Kansas City 1970
Silver gelatin print on paper

Sony cassette recorder by Warhol superstar Bridget Berlin and later came out as 'Live at Max's' (1972). They were great. Too great.

The problem maybe was that New York was a decade or so ahead of the rest of the country. I always thought that time started out in Time Square and then filtered through Jersey toward the rubes who were the great marketplace of America. The big bands had names like Kansas, Black Oak Arkansas, Alabama, Boston Chicago. What does that tell you? Record execs knew that New York bands were too far out. And the truth is that New York was different. Johnny Carson made jokes about New York being dangerous every night on the 'Tonight Show' and in New York even the hippies were scary. And so a music scene evolved that made music not for America or for the world but for New York. The punk scene and the glam scene that came before it was music made to amuse yourself and your friends. The musicians had ambition, but like that of a kid who says he wants to be a movie star when he grows up. In reality it would be satisfying enough to be famous in the East Village. And so New York musicians began to be themselves.

In the big world of rock and roll, musicians tended to look like richer versions of their audience – hippies with cash – but New Yorkers understood that this was show business and so they dressed for the stage. It's true that New York had its own hippies, but it wasn't Haight-Ashbury. New York hippies promoted peace and love but carried knives. New York's hipsters were streetwise, and you saw a lot of them, of all races and sexes. Most of all you saw personality and attitude. And sex. New York was always about sex and drugs. And then rock and roll. The primal New York glam scene revolved around the Mercer Arts Center. The bands you found there were freaks: the Magic Tramps, Ruby and the Rednecks, the New York Dolls, Harlots, Tuff Darts, Teenage Lust and the Lustettes, Suicide, Luger (whose guitarist was Ivan Kral), Rags, Wayne County, Street Punk, and Sniper, whose lead singer later became Joey Ramone.

It wasn't called glam. It wasn't called punk. (Punk wasn't even called punk until it was over.) It was just New York rock and roll, but it cobbled together a unique aesthetic. The media didn't really call it glam either. They called it glitter rock, by which they meant reformed hippies in glitter, eye make-up and some spandex with platform shoes, playing rock with fewer solos and more ambiguous lyrics. It was young heterosexual men like the New York Dolls taking their style tips from Times Square transvestites and Third Avenue male hustlers. After all, outrage is outrage. It was akin to the way Hell's Angels and Sicilian mafiosi would kiss on the lips to shock outsiders and affirm their outsider solidarity.

The Rolling Stones were pioneers of sexual ambivalence. Mick Jagger went Liz Taylor in Donald Cammell and Nicolas Roeg's proto-glam film Performance (produced in 1968, but not released until 1970), while the band appeared in drag for the cover of their 1966 single 'Have You Seen Your Mother, Baby, Standing in the Shadow?' But the New York Dolls took it to another level, almost caricaturing the Stones. David Johansen and Johnny Thunders, singer and guitarist respectively, were like a hooker drag queen version of Mick and Keith, with full lipstick and mascara, teased hair, and platform boots. They would carry this Quaalude vision across the seas.

Shock was also the motive of Alice Cooper, who had moved to New York from Detroit, enacting his own polymorphously perverse vision. With Cooper, America finally responded to glam. The New York Dolls and the Ramones toured the United Kingdom and we got punk. But the glam lend lease worked both ways, and gave both sides of the ocean a 'next level' to which to aspire. Iggy Pop and Lou Reed toured the UK, while America got David Bowie and T. Rextasy and Mott the Hoople and... uh... Jobriath, a gay-rock trial balloon, sadly shot down by a square and unready record industry, and 'Johnny Cougar', the pre-career of John Mellencamp, who was managed by Bowie's manager Tony DeFries. There was also Gary Glitter, whose 'Rock and Roll Part 2' (1972) was huge in the gay discos of New York.

New York hipsters knew that British glam rock was the capons coming home to roost. We had started it all with Warhol's Factory, with Jack Smith (with films such as *Flaming Creatures* and *Normal Love*, both from 1963), the Ballet Trockadero and the legendary Theatre of the Ridiculous, which was founded in 1965. With an assist from Detroit and its silver-painted topless blue-jeans boy Iggy Pop, and from San Francisco's Cockettes troupe. The Theatre of the Ridiculous was seminal. John Vaccaro directed, Ronald Tavel (also a Warhol scenarist) wrote plays. Charles Ludlam also wrote and starred and the casts included Factory superstars Jackie Curtis (also a playwright), Candy Darling, Mary Woronov, Taylor Meade, Ondine and Ultra Violet, Jack Smith superstar Mario Montez, Wayne/Jayne County and Ruby Lynn Reyner (of Ruby and the Rednecks), and even Patti Smith. They created the glam aesthetic. Bowie associate Leee 'Black' Childers believes that John Vaccaro was responsible for the glitter craze: 'People had been wearing glitter for a long time and the drag queens were wearing it on the street, but I think "glitter" really took off when John Vaccaro went shopping for costume material [...] He came across this little place in Chinatown that was having a big clearance sale on their glitter. He bought it all – giant shopping bag-size bags of glitter in all colours.'[1]

While Andy Warhol's personal glamour was more by reflection: he was a highly polished surface and he knew precisely whom to reflect. His philosophy is best expressed in his view of the Factory, that he was hanging around his entourage, they weren't hanging around him. He knew that if he couldn't magnetise personally he could put together an entourage that could. Warhol was the master impresario of outness and he knew precisely when and where to borrow the most relevant and newsworthy forms of infra-glamour, sampling the best ideas and talent from a broad palette and turning them into meta-glamour.

The Factory glam aesthetic was a heady mix of high fashion and society (Baby Jane Holzer, Edie Sedgwick, Ultra Violet and Susan Bottomly), modern dance via the Judson Dance Theater, rock via the Velvet Underground and Nico, male hustler macho stud (Joe Dallesandro, Louis Waldon, Eric Emerson), and campy drag queens (borrowed and adopted from filmmaker and artist Jack Smith, who coined the term 'Superstar', and the Theatre of the Ridiculous.) Warhol cashed in big time on the outrageous aesthetic and spirit of both Smith and the Theatre of the Ridiculous, creating a somewhat more commercially palatable presentation which he harnessed on film and also exported to London with his incredibly influential if non-money making play *Pork* (1971). The play and its cast were so successful in London that, following its run at the Roundhouse in Camden Town, David Bowie and Tony Defries hired the entire cast to run the New York office of Mainman Inc.

If Andy Warhol was the most glam artist, he thought that the most glam artists were Ray Johnson, David Hockney and Jack Smith. Jack was glam in a trash can, while Ray was glam in a vacuum: icily cooler and more distant and cute than Warhol even. Glam aspires to ivory towers. Iciness was an essential quality of glam. *Noli mi tangere*. Glam bands didn't have stage divers. David Bowie got that cold thing. It's all over the song he wrote 'Andy Warhol'. I was at the Factory the day Bowie came up to sing it to Andy. Andy asked me if we should let him in. Andy thought Bowie's long hair was boring. The following week I had mine cut. Soon after so did Bowie. Like Warhol, Bowie was a master borrower. He borrowed from Warhol in the way Warhol borrowed from Vaccaro and Smith. Glam went global and mainstream via Bowie, who became a veritable conglomerate of glam with the appropriations from Warhol and with the subsidiaries Lou Reed and Iggy Pop.

Another vision of glam arrived from San Francisco in November 1971 with the Cockettes, a sort of transgender hippie commune on an acid and glitter trip. The entire 47 person troupe arrived from San Francisco, bringing

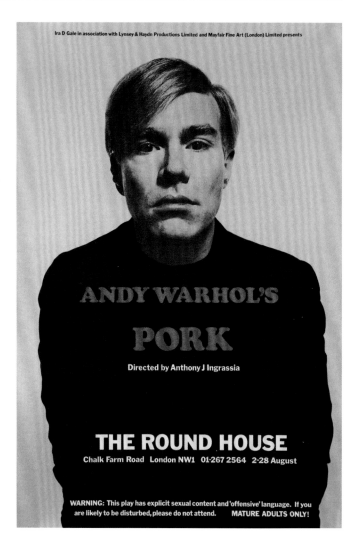

Above. Billy Sullivan
Sirpa, St. Regis Hotel, New York 1975

Left: Billy Sullivan
Wayne County, London 1971

Opposite: Andy Warhol
Andy Warhol's PORK 1971
Screenprinted poster on paper

Above: Leandro Katz
Turds in Hell (Stigmata) 1969/2003
Digital print on watercolour paper

Right: Billy Sullivan
Andrea Feldman, Jackie Curtis and Rita Reid, West 87th Street, New York 1970

Opposite: Cockettes – GTO's – The Stooges 1971
Printed poster on metallised paper

their own hippie version of glam with their review *Tinsel Tarts in a Hot Coma* to the Anderson Theatre in the East Village. Although the Cockettes were a social hit – it seemed that Alejandro Jodorowsky left his wife for one of the non-bearded ones – their performance was a spectacular flop. New Yorkers expected even degenerates to be professional. Gore Vidal quipped: 'Having no talent is not enough.' The Cockettes did prove to have some talent, however, in the form of a large black transvestite named Sylvester, who disavowed the troupe and went solo after several performances. Forming the Hot Band, he went on to make eleven glam albums before his AIDS-related death in 1988.

Meanwhile, since the late 1960s John Waters had been working in the showbiz Siberia of Baltimore, Maryland, melding glam attitudes with sleaze aesthetics and nihilist humour in his extraordinary films. He emerged into the slime-light in 1972 with *Pink Flamingos*, which plumbed the dark side of glam. Waters became a staple of the new institution of midnight movies – cult films screened in the hours when theatres were usually dark to audiences. Waters' clan (which resembled a Warhol Factory version of the Manson Family) settled into New York culture, providing an amusing conflation of glamour, fame and crime. Divine, wielding a gun and starring as Dawn Davenport, summed up the Waters philosophy in the denouement of his 1974 film *Female Trouble*: 'Take a good look at me because I'm going to be on the front of every newspaper in the country tomorrow! You're looking at crime personified and don't you forget it... And I'm so fucking beautiful I can't stand it myself! Now everybody freeze. Who wants to be famous? Who wants to die for art?'

So much for philosophy. Sensationalism was established in the cultural capitals, but the ultimate midnight movie would take it to the farthest reaches of the media, the cultural hinterlands. *The Rocky Horror Picture Show*, a 1975 film based on the 1973 London stage production, became a global ritual as audiences dressed up as their favourite characters, regardless of gender, revealing hitherto unexplored depths of bent identity pervading middle-class youth. I remember youth taking the transgender glam into unsuspecting suburban cinemas, thousands of confused long-haired rock and roll youths sang the Bowie-penned lyrics of 'All the Young Dudes' along with Mott the Hoople: 'Now I've drunk a lot of wine and I'm feeling fine got to race some cat to bed.' The revolution was underway. Today those young dudes are married, some to each other.

The tragedy of glam was that many of its most glittering stars died young (Candy Darling, Jackie Curtis, Jobriath, Eric Emerson, Johnny Thunders, Klaus Nomi and Marc Bolan) or didn't attain the altitude they deserved. Instead glam became Kiss (releasing four solo albums in one day) and heavy metal bands pretending to be drag queens. For me, the seminal moment of glam triumph was Wayne County with twinkle lights in her hair kicking the ass of Handsome Dick Manitoba of the Dictators, who had drunkenly heckled her ('Homo!'). Glam bam thank you ma'am. The glitter still hasn't really settled yet.

1 Legs McNeil and Gillian McCain, eds., *Please Kill Me: The Uncensored Oral History of Punk*, New York: Penguin Books, 1996, p. 88.

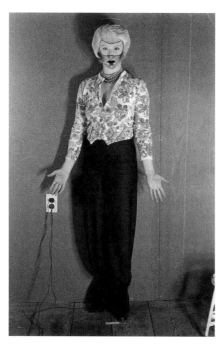
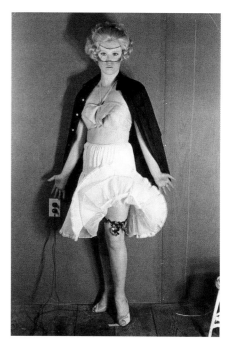
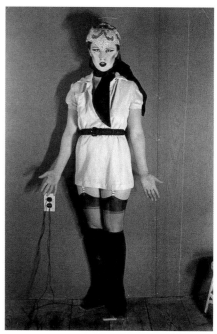
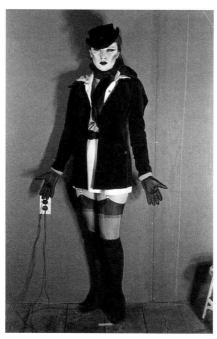
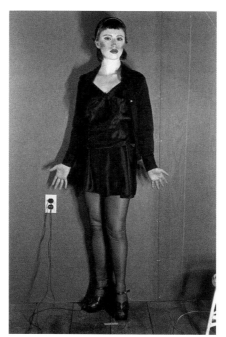

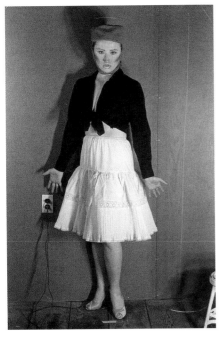

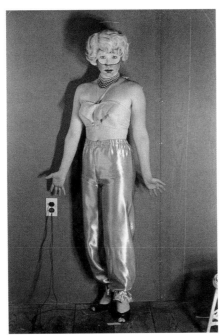

Cindy Sherman
Untitled (Line-Up) 1977/2011
Photographs on paper

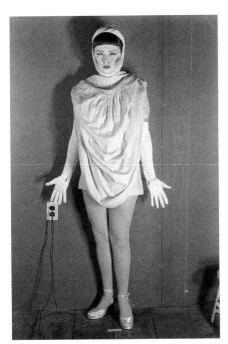

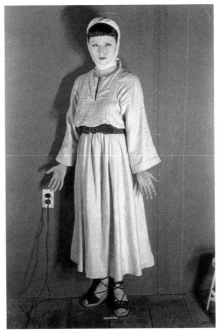

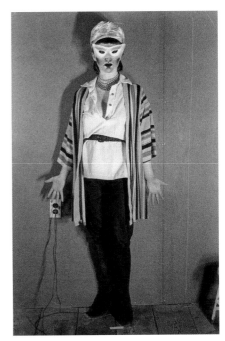

After Transformer

Jean-Christophe Ammann

Transformer was the title of a touring exhibition staged in 1974 during my curatorship at the Kunstmuseum Luzern. It brought together works by Katharina Sieverding, Jürgen Klauke, Urs Lüthi and Luigi Ontani and others, presented alongside rock and pop performers of the era, including Mick Jagger, Brian Eno and The New York Dolls. The exhibition, though, was just the tip of the iceberg, and was rooted in the period after 1968, a time of fluid gender transitions and diffusions in the realm of popular culture, which were also evident in visual art and performance. At this time the body was always one thing and another: both male and female, yet in people were only ever talking about the male body! For a short while this active ambiguity was demonstratively exposed. The removal of barriers was expansive and creative. The crucial point was that the blatantly physical interaction had an erotic edge and was publicly ritualised.

Jürgen Klauke
Transformer (detail) 1973
Three photographs on paper

To quote David Johansen, lead singer of The New York Dolls, when I interviewed him in 1973: 'Whenever I dress and move in this particular way, provocation becomes that much more provocative, aggression becomes more aggressive, the masculine side all the more masculine and the feminine side more feminine.'

During a conversation in 1973, Brian Eno, a member of Roxy Music at the time, jotted down – on the spur of the moment – his masculine and feminine sides:

sexy	*female*
insane	*male*
grotesque	*female*
sinister	*male*
beautiful	*female*
passionate	*female*
incessant	*m / f*
desperate	*male*
angular	*m / f*
reptilian	*female*

It was only later that I came to understand that men have more feminine traits than women have masculine traits – they have a 'specific' feminine side which, traditionally, has always been suppressed and only really came to light after 1968. Women benefited from that symbolic year. Before 1968 – not to put too fine a point on it – there was still women's art. After 1968 there were women artists. After 1968 women no longer tried to discover and develop their masculine side, but concentrated instead on their specifically feminine side – the part that had been suppressed during the course of the 'history of women'.

Transformer spoke of a limited expanse of time. That time was one big party. But every party has to come to an end. The bright light that burnt in those days made an impact – cognitively and experientially. What was provocative back then became part of daily life (metrosexuality and queerdom). And the gay pride parades were no less a party, with tens of thousands of young people joining with gay men and women. But the bright light of back then has changed into, let's say, everyday normality. The phenomenon 'Jeff Koons' is a perfect example of this. In 1992, when I wrote a book about, and with, Jeff Koons (published by Taschen), pornography was still regarded as provocative. The book contained images of Koons engaging in anal penetration with his then partner Cicciolina, a Hungarian-born porn star. In 2012, in the catalogue for a solo exhibition Koons himself has censored the dicks and the pussies. As on Pay TV in American hotel rooms, people are seen shagging with not a glimpse of

Cindy Sherman
Cover Girls (Vogue) 1976
Three photographs on paper

Opposite, top: *Transformer* catalogue 1974

Opposite, below: Eleanor Antin
The King 1972

so
gesehen
wie
ich
dich
sehe

so
gesehen
wie
du
mich
siehst

DEZEMBER'73   ULAY

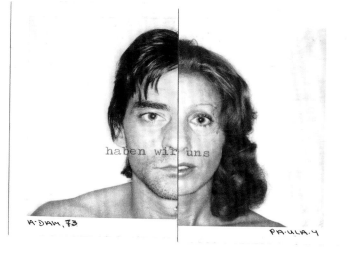

haben wir uns

A·DAM, 73   PA·ULA·Y

Far left, top to bottom: Ulay
S'he 1972
Three Auto-Polaroids

Left, top to bottom:
PA-ULA-Y 1974
Three Auto-Polaroids with montage and text

Top: Ulay
PA-ULA-Y 1973
The Auto-Polaroids (from the series Renais sense)

Right: Ulay
Untitled 1972

Bernd Janssen
Untitled (Sigmar Polke in Willich) 1973
Photograph on paper

Above: Sigmar Polke
Kandinsdingsda (Wir Kleinbürger), 1976
Gouache, acrylic and collage on paper mounted on canvas

Left: Sigmar Polke, Achim Duchow, Astrid Heibach and Katharina Steffen
Day after Day... They Take Some Brain Away 1975
Published on the occasion of the 1975 São Paulo Biennial

Jürgen Klauke
Transformer 1973
Three photographs on paper

the main attraction. Why has he done that? It is because these days pornography has become common currency through the Internet. And through being common currency now, this act of 'self-censorship' twenty years later is a deliberate artistic act.

The exhibition *Transformer* and Lou Reed's 'Walk on the Wild Side' have become part of history. But the images live on, especially photographs. Documents and images: the two are distinguished by the fact that an image is always also a document, but a document need not always be an image. In that sense images from back then have become icons of an ecstatic take on life.

And also, not least, there is the matter of desire. It is one of the parameters of Western art. Is Jeff Koons' 'self-censorship' justified artistically? Eroticism and sensuality have always been connected with the human body. But we also find sensuality in Piet Mondrian's Constructivist paintings. Due to the ongoing mediafication of the erotic and sexual body, art is drifting deeper and deeper into 'research'. By 'research' I mean resorting to socio-econonic and eco-feminist strategies. In the case of *Transformer*, this means that the body as a form of desire reflecting on itself is disappearing from art. Instead, the body as a stronghold of sensuality and eroticism, laden with radical potential, is becoming a test-bed for research-based practices. The question for us now is whether or not this is the future of art.

GLAM
The
Performance
of Style

TIMELINE

Jonathan Harris and Barry Curtis

POLITICS & SOCIETY

- Broadcast of weekly pop music television show *Top of the Pops* begins on 1 January 1964
- Susan Sontag's 'Notes on "Camp": A Modern Sensibility' is published in *Partisan Review*

ART

- David Hockney dances with Derek Jarman at the Slade School of Fine Art's Christmas dance
- Bryan Ferry studies Fine Art under Richard Hamilton at Newcastle University
- Andy Warhol's film *Mario Banana* starring Mario Montez
- Billy Name silvers the walls of Warhol's Factory

FASHION & STYLE

- Bermans & Nathans, the theatrical outfitters, supply the Kinks with pink hunting jackets, breeches and frilled shirts
- Mary Quant and Vicky Tiel invent the miniskirt in London and New York respectively
- Biba boutique is opened by Barbara Hulanicki in Abingdon Road, Kensington, London

FILM & THEATRE

- Featuring Nazi costumes and occult themes, *Scorpio Rising* directed by Kenneth Anger is seized by Vice Squad at its premiere, but is then approved by California Supreme Court

MUSIC

- David Bowie is in succession of bands including the King Bees, the Mannish Boys and the Lower Third
- George Hunter and the Charlatans pop group forms in San Francisco, wearing Victorian clothes and aiming for 'a sort of unisex, android' identity

POLITICS & SOCIETY

ART

FASHION & STYLE

FILM & THEATRE

MUSIC

1965

1966

POLITICS & SOCIETY

1966
- First lunar orbit achieved by NASA
- Harold Wilson leads the Labour Party to win the general election in the United Kingdom

ART

- Andy Warhol meets Ultra Violet and Edie Sedgwick, makes *Silver Clouds*, and starts managing the Velvet Underground
- Joseph Beuys performs *How to Explain Art to a Dead Hare* with gold leaf and honey on his face

- Aubrey Beardsley exhibition at the Victoria and Albert Museum
- Warhol launches the Exploding Plastic Inevitable events series and directs *Chelsea Girls* with Paul Morrissey – his first commercial success, described as 'Three and a half hours of split screen improvisation, poorly photographed, hardly edited at all, employing perversion and sensation'

FASHION & STYLE

- Michael Fish opens Mr Fish boutique in Clifford Street
- Granny Takes a Trip opens at 488 King's Road, London, and is visited by Ossie Clark and Andy Warhol
- *Time* magazine article by Shel Silverstein on 'Swinging London'.
- *Nova* magazine launched, edited by Molly Parkin

FILM & THEATRE

- *13 Most Beautiful Women*, *My Hustler* and *Vinyl* (a filmed rendition of the novel *A Clockwork Orange* by Anthony Burgess, 1962) made by Andy Warhol and his assistants
- Experimental theatre group The Play-House of the Ridiculous is founded in New York, later becoming the Theatre of the Ridiculous

- *Modesty Blaise*, directed by Joseph Losey, is vilified by reviewers, one describing it as 'painfully camp'

MUSIC

- Peter Whitehead directs a promotional film for the Rolling Stones' single 'Have You Seen Your Mother, Baby, Standing in the Shadow?', in which the band appear in 1940s drag
- 'Dedicated Follower of Fashion' released by the Kinks
- Mickey Ruskin opens the nightclub Max's Kansas City, 213 Park Avenue South, New York, which becomes a hang-out for Andy Warhol and New York's avant-garde

1965

1966

1967

- Sexual Offences Act decriminalises male homosexuality in the UK
- Far right National Front party founded in the United Kingdom

1968

- Student riots in France, the United States and Poland, and in the United Kingdom at Hornsey College of Art and the London School of Economics
- Riots following police raid at Stonewall Tavern in New York signal the beginning of the Gay Rights movement
- Disruption of Miss America beauty contest by feminists

- Peter Blake and Jann Haworth design the album cover for *Sgt Pepper's Lonely Hearts Club Band* by the Beatles

- Lindsay Kemp performs at the Edinburgh Festival, later works with David Bowie
- Attempt to assassinate Andy Warhol by Valerie Solanas
- Richard Hamilton's *Swingeing London 67* series of paintings emblematises the coming together of pop music and visual art

- Ossie Clark's first fashion show for Radley at Chelsea Town Hall, filmed by Pathé
- John Stephens opens a chain of shops on Carnaby Street, bringing fashion to the masses
- Zandra Rhodes and Sylvia Ayton open Fulham Road Clothes Shop

- Antony Price graduates from the Royal College of Art, London, starts designing clothes for Stirling Cooper

- *Bonnie and Clyde*, directed by Arthur Penn, inspires a wave of interest in 1930s fashion

- *2001: A Space Odyssey* directed by Stanley Kubrick
- *Barbarella* directed by Roger Vadim

- The Velvet Underground's debut album produced by Andy Warhol

- Pan's People dance troupe (formed in 1966) first appear on *Top of the Pops*
- MC5 debut album *Kick Out the Jams* is released

1969

POLITICS & SOCIETY

- First colour broadcasts on British television
- Apollo 11 mission lands on the moon
- Richard Nixon becomes President of the United States
- British troops sent to Northern Ireland

ART

- Gilbert & George graduate from St. Martins School of Art as Singing Sculpture
- Franz Gertsch makes his first large hyper-realistic painting

- *Pop Art Redefined* exhibition at the Hayward Gallery, London, includes a jukebox curated by artist Mark Lancaster
- Allen Jones begins making fetishistic 'women as furniture' artworks

FASHION & STYLE

- Alkasura boutique opened by John Lloyd at 304 King's Road
- Keith, hairstylist to Roxy Music circle, opens a shop in Knightsbridge
- Tommy Roberts and Trevor Myles open Mr Freedom, 430 King's Road

- Antony Price and Juliet Mann open Che Guevara boutique, Kensington High Street, London

FILM & THEATRE

- *Performance*, directed by Nic Roeg and Donald Cammell, about the performative turn in music and crime, coincides with trial of gangsters the Kray Twins

- *The Damned*, directed by Luigi Visconti, is the first of the director's 'German trilogy', followed by *Death in Venice* (1971) and *Ludwig* (1973). It portrays the Nazi 'Night of the Long Knives' as a gangster massacre and homosexual orgy

MUSIC

- The Mothers of Invention, led by Frank Zappa, dress in drag for the cover of their album *We're Only in it for the Money*, a parody of the cover of the Beatles' *Sgt Pepper's Lonely Hearts Club Band*
- David Bowie's 'Space Oddity' is top of United Kingdom singles charts
- Rolling Stones' free concert, Hyde Park, London
- The Stooges debut album is recorded

1969

1970

- Protest by feminists at Miss World contest at the Royal Albert Hall
- Equal pay for women becomes law in the United Kingdom
- Contraceptive pill available to all women through family planning clinics
- In the United Kingdom between 1970 and 1974 nearly 3,000 strikes and 14 million days lost to industrial action

- Margaret Harrison founds Women's Liberation Art Group; exhibition of her work features image of Hugh Hefner as a naked Bunny Girl
- Judy Chicago changes her name and appears as a boxer for her show at California State University. She also starts first feminist art programme at Fresno State College
- Police raid Open Space, London, and confiscate Andy Warhol's film *Flesh*
- Miss General Idea pageant, St. Lawrence Center for the Arts, Toronto

- Italian *Vogue* runs a spread titled 'Il Mondo di Max's Kansas City' (The World of Max's Kansas City')

- Mike Sarne directs *Myra Breckenridge*, an adaptation of Gore Vidal's novel featuring Mae West and Raquel Welch which is described by critic Dennis Altman as 'a cultural assault on assumed norms'

- Marc Bolan shortens the name of his group from Tyrannosaurus Rex to T. Rex, signalling a move away from acoustic whimsy towards chart-friendly rock and roll
- The Kinks release 'Lola', a song detailing a romantic encounter in a nightclub between a man and a transvestite or transgendered person
- David Bowie releases the album *The Man Who Sold the World*

1970

1971

• Gay Liberation Front meeting at Middle Earth, Covent Garden, London

• David Hockney paints *Mr and Mrs Clark and Percy* – portrait of designers Ossie Clark and Celia Birtwell
• Annette Messager begins *The Collector*, a series of self-portraits exploring media images of feminity
• David Bowie meets Andy Warhol and his entourage at the Factory, New York
• Steve Arnold directs *Luminess Procuress*

• Malcolm McLaren and Vivienne Westwood open Let it Rock at 430 King's Road, London, selling 1950s revivalist fashion
• Hot pants and platform heels appear in many fashion magazines
• *Esquire* magazine features an article 'The Politics of the Costume', showing Jackie Curtis (the transvestite star of Warhol films) posing at a New York boutique wearing a bodice belonging to Lana Turner and feathers once owned by Marlene Dietrich
• Kansai Yamamoto fashion show held in London

• Jim Jacobs and Warren Casey stage the musical *Grease*, set in 1959, at Kingston Mines Theatre, Chicago
• Ken Russell directs *The Boyfriend*, a camp musical extravaganza set in the 1920s and featuring Twiggy
• Stanley Kubrick directs *A Clockwork Orange*

• T. Rex perform 'Hot Love' on Top of the Pops; it tops the charts for six weeks. Shortly before filming commences, Chelita Secunda adds spots of glitter to Marc Bolan's cheeks. T. Rex are the bestselling singles group of the year
• Alice Cooper releases the album *Love It To Death*

1971

1972

- *Gay News* founded to mark the first Gay Pride march
- *Spare Rib* feminist magazine founded
- Eugene Cernan in Apollo 17 is the last man to walk on the moon
- 'Page 3' topless photographs of women become a regular feature in newspaper *The Sun*
- The Watergate scandal breaks in the United States
- *The Joy of Sex*, a popular sex manual by Alex Comfort, is published

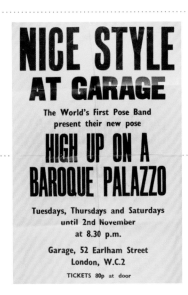

NICE STYLE
AT GARAGE

The World's First Pose Band
present their new pose

HIGH UP ON A
BAROQUE PALAZZO

Tuesdays, Thursdays and Saturdays
until 2nd November
at 8.30 p.m.

Garage, 52 Earlham Street
London, W.C.2

TICKETS 80p at door

- Nice Style: The World's First Pose Band is formed by Garry Chitty, Robin Fletcher, Bruce McLean and Paul Richards
- Marc Camille Chaimowicz's *Celebration? Real Life* is shown at Sigi Krauss Gallery, London, with soundtrack featuring David Bowie and others
- Eleanor Antin's *The King* shows experimentation with masculine appearances

- Rodney Bingenheimer opens glam rock club The English Disco in Los Angeles
- Willie and Mel Walters open Swanky Modes in Camden Town, London
- Tommy Roberts opens City Lights in Floral Street, Covent Garden, London

- *Cabaret*, directed by Bob Fosse, is released
- John Waters directs *Pink Flamingos* starring Divine, an actor and drag artist who had previously appeared in Waters' 1969 film *Mondo Trasho*

- Cover of Roxy Music's eponymous first album is photographed by Nick de Ville and styled by Antony Price
- David Bowie christens his backing band 'The Spiders from Mars'. The Ziggy Stardust look is unveiled when the group performs on *The Old Grey Whistle Test*, and later 'Starman' is performed on *Top of the Pops*
- Lou Reed's *Transformer* album is produced by David Bowie and Mick Ronson
- The 'Rock and Roll Show' at Wembley Stadium features Bill Haley, MC5, Gary Glitter and others

1972

1973

POLITICS & SOCIETY

- The Irish Republican Army begins mainland bombing campaign in the United Kingdom
- The feminist publisher Virago is founded
- Miners' strike in the United Kingdom

ART

- Bruce McLean's 'Contemporary Pose' lecture at Royal College of Art, London
- *Transformer* by Jürgen Klauke shows images of the artist which question the role of masculinity
- *Transformer* by Katharina Sieverding presents multi-layered androgynous portraits
- Nan Goldin has her first exhibition of photographs of New York's gay and transsexual community
- Destroy All Monsters band is formed – Mike Kelley, Jim Shaw, Cary Loren and Niagara present performances accompanied by mixed media collages

FASHION & STYLE

- Manon Boutique opens in Zürich and Manon makes her first Fetishbild
- *Cosmopolitan* launched in the United Kingdom – termed 'A Playboy for Women'
- Big Biba opens in Kensington High Street, London, with lavish Art Deco interiors designed by Whitmore-Thomas. The New York Dolls play in the restaurant, the Rainbow Room

FILM & THEATRE

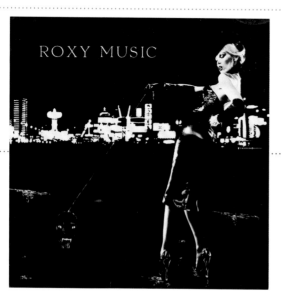

- The novel *Glam* by Richard Allen is published in the New English Library
- Jack Hazan directs *A Bigger Splash*, inspired by David Hockney's Los Angeles swimming pool paintings

MUSIC

- The New York Dolls' debut LP is released
- Jobriath releases eponymous debut album

1973

1974

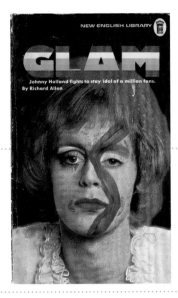

- Richard Nixon resigns and Gerald Ford becomes President of the United States
- Harold Wilson heads a new Labour Government
- The United Kingdom experiences power cuts and the three-day week due to industrial action

• Lynda Benglis's *Invitation* showing the artist nude with a dildo is produced in November's Artforum
• Nancy Hellebrand's *Londoners at Home* photographs feature 'glam rock' fans
• Jean-Christophe Ammann curates *Transformer* exhibition at Kunsthalle Luzern, Switzerland, exploring gender ambiguity in art in the context of glam rock

- McLaren and Westwood transform Let it Rock into Sex
- *The Fabric of Pop* exhibition is held at the Victoria and Albert Museum, London

• *The Great Gatsby*, an adaption of F.Scott Fitzgerald novel, is directed by Jack Clayton, featuring 1920s costumes designed by Ralph Lauren
• Michael Apted directs *Stardust* starring David Essex

• Cockney Rebel release 'Mr Soft' as a single
• Mud's 'Tiger Feet' and Alvin Stardust's 'Jealous Mind' reach number one in the United Kingdom singles charts

1974

1975

1976

POLITICS & SOCIETY

1975
- Margaret Thatcher triumphs in the Conservative leadership election

1976
- Britain applies to the International Monetary Fund for a £2.3 billion bail-out, resulting in austerity measures and spending cuts

ART

- Lindsay Kemp directs an all-male production of Oscar Wilde's *Salome* at the Roundhouse, London
- Lucy Lippard's essay 'Making Up, Role Playing and Transformation in Women's Art' is published in the collection of her essays *From the Center*

FASHION & STYLE

- Guy Bourdin takes fetishistic shoe photos for Charles Jourdan
- *File* magazine's 'Glamour Issue' by General Idea

FILM & THEATRE

- *The Man Who Fell to Earth*, directed by Nick Roeg, stars David Bowie as an androgynous alien
- Derek Jarman directs *Sebastiane*

MUSIC

- 'S-S-S-Single Bed' is a top five hit for Fox, fronted by Marlene Dietrich-styled singer Noosha Fox
- T. Rex have their last Top 40 hit with 'I Love to Boogie'

1975

1976

BIBLIOGRAPHY

Amaya, Mario, *Art Nouveau*, London: Studio Vista, 1966.

Ammann, Jean-Christophe, *Transformer: Aspekte der Travestie,* exh. cat., Kunstmuseum Luzern, 1974.

Auslander, Philip, *Performing Glam Rock: Gender and Theatricality in Popular Music*, Ann Arbor, Michigan: University of Michigan Press, 2006.

Ballard, J.G., *Concrete Island*, London: Jonathan Cape, 1974.

_____, *High Rise*, London: Jonathan Cape, 1975.

Baudelaire, Charles, *Selected Writings on Art and Literature*, trans. P. E. Charvet, London: Viking, 1972.

Beckett, Andy, *When the Lights Went Out: Britain in the Seventies*, London: Faber & Faber, 2009.

Bockris, Victor, *Warhol*, Harmondsworth: Penguin, 1989.

Booker, Christopher, *The Neophiliacs: A Study of the Revolution in English Life in the Fifties and Sixties*, London: Collins, 1969.

Bourdieu, Pierre, *Distinction: A Social Critique of the Judgement of Taste*, London: Routledge, 1986.

Bracewell, Michael, *Remake/Remodel: Art, Pop, Fashion and the Making of Roxy Music, 1953–1972*, London: Faber & Faber, 2007.

_____, *England is Mine: Pop Life in Albion*, London: Faber & Faber, 2009.

Breward, Christopher, *Fashioning London: Clothing and the Modern Metropolis*, London: Berg, 2004.

Brown, Norman O., *Life Against Death: The Psychoanalytical Meaning of History*, Middletown, CT: Wesleyan University Press, 1959.

_____, *Love's Body*, New York: Vintage Books, 1966.

Buckley, David, *Strange Fascination: David Bowie: The Definitive Story*, London: Virgin, 2000.

_____, *The Thrill of It All: The Story of Bryan Ferry and Roxy Music*, London: Andre Deutsch, 2004.

Butler, Judith, *Gender Trouble: Feminism and the Subversion of Identity*, London: Routledge, 1990.

Cann, Kevin, *David Bowie: Any Day Now, the London Years (1947–1974)*, London: Adelita, 2010.

Cole, Shaun, *Don We Now Our Gay Apparel: Gay Men's Dress in the Twentieth Century*, Oxford and New York: Berg, 2000.

Cooper, David, ed., *The Dialectics of Liberation*, London: Penguin, 1967.

Core, Philip, *The Original Eye: Arbiters of Twentieth Century Taste*, Englewood Cliffs, New Jersey: Prentice Hall, 1984.

Crisp, Quentin, *How to Have a Life-style*, London: Cecil Woolf, 1975.

Debord, Guy, *The Society of the Spectacle*, Detroit: Black and Red, 1970.

Décharné, Max, *King's Road: The Rise and Fall of the Hippest Street in the World*, London: Weidenfeld & Nicolson, 2005.

Doggett, Peter, *The Man Who Sold The World: David Bowie and the 1970s*, London: Bodley Head, 2011.

Dorfles, Gillo, *Kitsch: The World of Bad Taste*, New York: Bell Publishing, 1968.

Farren, Mick and Ed Barker, *Watch Out Kids*, London: Open Gate Books, 1972.

Foster, Hal and Alex Bacon, *Richard Hamilton*, London: MIT Press, 2010.

Fountain, Nigel, *Underground: The London Alternative Press 1966–74*, London: Routledge, 1988.

Frith, Simon, *Sound Effects: Youth, Leisure, and the Politics of Rock 'n' Roll*, New York: Pantheon Books, 1981.

Frith, Simon and Howard Horne, *Art into Pop*, London: Methuen, 1987.

Gill, John, *Queer Noises: Male and Female Homosexuality in Twentieth-Century Music*, London: Cassell, 1995.

Gorman, Paul, *Mr. Freedom: Tommy Roberts, British Design Hero*, London: Adelita, 2012.

_____, *The Look: Adventures in Pop and Rock Fashion*, London: Sanctuary, 2001.

Green, Jonathon, *Days in the Life: Voices from the English Underground 1961–1971*, London: Heinemann, 1988.

Hackett, Pat, *POPism: The Warhol Sixties*, New York: Harcourt Brace Jovanovich, 1980.

Hall, Stuart and Tony Jefferson, eds., *Resistance through Rituals: Youth Subcultures in Postwar Britain*, London: Routledge, 1993.

Hamilton, Richard, *Collected Words*, London: Thames & Hudson, 1983.

Hebdige, Dick, *Subculture: The Meaning of Style*, London: Methuen, 1979.

Hewison, Robert, *Too Much: Art & Society in the Sixties, 1960–75*, London: Methuen, 1986.

Hillier, Bevis, *Art Deco*, London: Studio Vista, 1968.

_____, *Austerity Binge: The Decorative Arts of the Forties and Fifties*, London: Studio Vista, 1975.

Hills, Matt, *Fan Cultures*, London: Routledge, 2002.

Hoskyns, Barney, *Glam! Bowie, Bolan and the Glitter Rock Revolution*, London: Faber & Faber, 1998.

Hulanicki, Barbara, *From A to Biba*, London: Hutchinson, 1983.

Inglis, Ian, ed., *Performance and Popular Music: History, Place and Time*, Aldershot: Ashgate, 2006.

Ironside, Janey, *A Fashion Alphabet*, London: Michael Joseph, 1968.

Isherwood, Christopher, *Goodbye to Berlin*, London: Hogarth Press, 1940.

Kracauer, Siegfried, trans. Thomas Y. Levin, *The Mass Ornament: Weimar Essays*, Cambridge, MA and London: Harvard University Press, 1995.

Laing, R. D., *The Politics of Experience*, New York: Pantheon, 1967.

Lewis, Lisa, ed., *The Adoring Audience: Fan Culture and Popular Media*,

BIBLIOGRAPHY (continued)

London: Routledge, 1992.

Lippard, Lucy, *From the Center: Feminist Essays on Women's Art*, New York: Plume, 1976.

Lutyens, Dominic and Kirsty Hislop, *70s Style and Design*, London: Thames & Hudson, 2009.

Martin, Bernice, *Sociology of Contemporary Cultural Change*, Oxford: Blackwell, 1981.

McNeil, Legs and Gillian McCain, eds., *Please Kill Me: The Uncensored Oral History of Punk*, New York: Penguin Books, 1996.

McRobbie, Angela, ed., *Zoot Suits and Second Hand Dresses: An Anthology of Fashion and Music*, Basingstoke: Macmillan, 1989.

_____, *Feminism and Youth Culture: From Jackie to Just Seventeen*, Basingstoke: Macmillan, 1991.

Melly, George, *Revolt into Style: The Pop Arts in Britain*, London: Allen Lane, 1970.

Miles, Barry, *In the Seventies: Adventures in the Counterculture*, London: Serpent's Tail, 2011.

Millett, Kate, *Sexual Politics*, Garden City, New York: Doubleday, 1970.

Mulholland, Neil, *The Cultural Devolution: Art in Britain in the Late Twentieth Century*, London: Ashgate, 2003.

Nelson, Elizabeth, *The British Counterculture 1966–73: A Study of the Underground Press*, London: Macmillan, 1989.

Neville, Richard, *Play Power*, London: Jonathan Cape, 1970.

Nuttall, Jeff, *Bomb Culture*, London: MacGibbon & Kee, 1968.

Parker, Rozsika and Griselda Pollock, eds., *Framing Feminism: Art and the Women's Movement (1970–1985)*, London and New York: Pandora, 1987.

Paytress, Mark, *Bolan: The Rise and Fall of a 20th-Century Superstar*, London: Omnibus, 2002.

Pincus-Witten, Robert, *Postminimalism into Maximalism: American Art 1966–1986*, Ann Arbor, Michigan: UMI Research Press, 1986.

Polhemus, Ted, *Fashion and Anti-Fashion: An Anthropology of Clothing and Adornment*, London: Thames & Hudson, 1978.

Proll, Astrid, ed., *Goodbye to London: Radical Art & Politics in the 70s*, Ostfildern: Hatje Cantz, 2010.

Raban, Jonathan, *Soft City: What Cities Do To Us, and How They Change The Way We Live, Think and Feel*, London: Hamish Hamilton, 1974.

Reynolds, Simon, *Retromania: Pop Culture's Addiction to its Own Past*, London: Faber & Faber, 2011.

Rock, Mick, *Glam! An Eyewitness Account*, London: Music Sales, 2005.

Ross, Geoffrey Aquilana, *The Day of the Peacock: Style for Men 1963–1973*, London: V&A Publications, 2011.

Rous, Lady Henrietta, ed., *The Ossie Clark Diaries*, London: Bloomsbury, 1988.

Rowe, Marsha, ed., *Spare Rib Reader*, Harmondsworth: Penguin, 1982.

Sandbrook, Dominic, *State of Emergency: The Way We Were, Britain 1970–1974*, London: Allen Lane, 2010.

Seago, Alex, *Burning the Box of Beautiful Things: The Development of a Postmodern Sensibility*, Oxford: Oxford University Press, 1995.

Shail, Robert, *Seventies British Cinema*, London: British Film Institute/Palgrave Macmillan, 2008.

Sheppard, David, *On Some Faraway Beach: The Life and Times of Brian Eno*, London: Orion, 2009.

Skurka, Norma and Gili Oberto, *Underground Interiors: Decorating for Alternative Lifestyles*, New York: Quadrangle, 1972.

Sontag, Susan. *Against Interpretation and Other Essays*, New York: Farrah Straus & Giroux, 1966.

Sounes, Howard, *Seventies: The Sights, Sounds and Ideas of a Brilliant Decade*, London: Simon & Schuster, 2006.

Students and Staff of Hornsey College of Art, *The Hornsey Affair*, Harmondsworth: Penguin, 1969.

Tamm, Eric, *Brian Eno: His Music and the Vertical Colour of Sound*, London: Faber & Faber, 1990.

Taylor, Marvin J., ed., *The Downtown Book: The New York Art Scene, 1974–1984*, Princeton, New Jersey: Princeton University Press, 2006.

Thompson, Dave, *Children of the Revolution: The Glam Rock Story, 1970–75*, London: Cherry Red, 2010.

Toffler, Alvin, *Future Shock: A Study of Mass Bewilderment in the Face of Accelerating Change*, New York: Bantam Books, 1970.

Turner, Alwyn, *Crisis? What Crisis? Britain in the 1970s*, London: Aurum, 2008.

_____, and Steven Thomas, *Big Biba: Inside the Most Beautiful Store in the World*, Woodbridge: Antique Collectors' Club, 2006.

Veronesi, Giulia, *Into the Twenties: Style and Design 1909–1929*, London: Thames and Hudson, 1968.

Visconti, Tony, *Bowie, Bolan and the Brooklyn Boy*, London: Harper, 2007.

Vyner, Harriet, *Groovy Bob: The Life and Times of Robert Fraser*, London: Faber & Faber, 1999.

Walker, John A., *Left Shift: Radical Art in 1970s Britain*, London: I.B. Tauris, 2002.

Walter, Aubrey, *Come Together: The Years of Gay Liberation 1970–73*, London: Gay Men's Press, 1980.

Warhol, Andy, *The Philosophy of Andy Warhol (from A to Z and Back Again)*, New York: Harcourt Brace Jovanovich, 1975.

Watt, Judith, *Ossie Clark 1965–1974*, London: V&A Publications, 2003.

York, Peter, *Style Wars*, London: Sidgwick & Jackson, 1980.

Compiled by Ron Moy with Darren Pih

TATE LIVERPOOL SUPPORTERS

Tate Liverpool thanks for their generous support

Sponsors and Donors
The American Patrons of Tate
The Art Fund
Biffa Award
Business in the Arts: North West
Culture Programme of the European Union
DLA Piper
Goethe-Institut London
Liverpool City Council
Liverpool City Council Parks & Green Spaces Department
Liverpool John Moores University
Liverpool Primary Care Trust
Liverpool Vision
LUMA Foundation
National Lottery through Arts Council England
Sky Arts
Tate Liverpool Members
U.S. Embassy, London
Winchester School of Art, University of Southampton

Corporate Partners
Christie's
David M Robinson (Jewellery) Ltd
DLA Piper
DWF
Liverpool & Sefton Health Partnership
Liverpool Hope University
Liverpool John Moores University
Peel Ports
Unilever UK
The University of Liverpool

Corporate Members
Andrew Collinge Ltd
Bruntwood
Cheetham Bell JWT
Deutsche Bank
Fraser Wealth Management
Grant Thornton
Hill Dickinson
Individual Restaurant Company Plc
Lime Pictures
Mazars
Rathbone Investment Management
Royal Bank of Scotland

Patrons
Elkan Abrahamson
Diana Barbour
David Bell
Lady Beverley Bibby
Jo & Tom Bloxham MBE
Bill Clark
Jim Davies
Olwen McLaughlin
Barry Owen OBE
Sue & Ian Poole
Anthony Preston
Alan Sprince

CREDITS